ZODIAC

ESSEX

Edited by Lucy Jeacock

First published in Great Britain in 2002 by
YOUNG WRITERS
Remus House,
Coltsfoot Drive,
Peterborough, PE2 9JX
Telephone (01733) 890066

HB ISBN 0 75433 548 8
SB ISBN 0 75433 549 6

FOREWORD

Young Writers was established in 1991 with the aim of promoting creative writing in children, to make reading and writing poetry fun.

Once again, this year proved to be a tremendous success with over 41,000 entries received nationwide.

The Zodiac competition has shown us the high standard of work and effort that children are capable of today. The competition has given us a vivid insight into the thoughts and experiences of today's younger generation. It is a reflection of the enthusiasm and creativity that teachers have injected into their pupils, and it shines clearly within this anthology.

The task of selecting poems was a difficult one, but nevertheless, an enjoyable experience. We hope you are as pleased with the final selection in *Zodiac Essex* as we are.

CONTENTS

Emma Willis	78
Elizabeth Brown	79
Nicholas Flynn	80
Daniel Ellis	80
Lisa Scott	81
Matthew O'Neill	82
Kelly Dalby	82
Lauren Pentelow	83
Michael Garside	84
Lauren Buckle	85
Rebecca Hadley	86
Ashley Jordan	86
Christina Fenn	87
James Wong	87
Coral Purcell	88
Nicholas Platt	88
Michael Edwards	89
Elliot Bishop	89
Thomas Shimali	90
Ben Gotch	90
Tom Thornton	90
Alexandra Wilson	91
Jake Nutley	91
Joe Read	91
William Simmons	92
Richard Gould	92
Megan Morris	93
Louise Smalley	93
Hannah Wells	94
James Stretch	95
Faye Moody	96
Dean Sambrook	97
Scott Wilkinson	98
Matthew Clark	98
Karen Bell	99
Alice Catherine Beatrice Feldwick	99
Danielle Lane	100

Great Baddow High School

Hassenbrook School

The Poems

BEACH

Sun setting above the glistening, still waters,
with the occasional lapping wave.
The sun causing an orange-blue clash.
the foamy horizon pin-pointed with a shiny white line.

The waters placidly smothering the golden crystals
that lay across the waters' bed
those crystals calmly lay,
and shining gently, white through ochre.

The more vapid of the motionless particles,
stake, hushed, colourless,
though comely and expensive
reflect the fading sun's rays.

The clear, blue stretch of glossy waters,
stifles the projected rocks,
giving echoes seemly as a wreckage
or an object being declined from a great height.

The sun lowers, as does the temperature,
soon proposing with it a docile wind.
Elevating the once still crystals,
and propelling them toward the horizon.

Leah Oaker (13)

THE QUESTION OF GOD...

God holds many questions,
Of which we'd like to ask,
The definition of himself
Is searched for in your heart.

It comes to you without fault,
With age you'll see it's true,
Imagination shall reveal,
The real god, that's just for you.

He'll be there by your side,
If ever in any doubt
He'll guide you through your lifetime
And catch you when you're falling.

However he may appear,
To you or anyone else,
His image serves no purpose,
Who? Whatever, he may be.

Just listen to his whisper,
Inside your head he'll be,
There for comfort, protection
        and support for you and me.

This therefore asks you
What God looks like
Don't hesitate to answer
The truth will lie inside.

Kay Heale

IMAGINE

Imagine a farm on the top of a hill,
And a carpet of fields all around it.
Imagine a woman poised with a quill,
And a mischievous blue-coated rabbit.

And you can imagine a sly, foxy gent
Who chatted up ladies wherever he went,
Like loveable Miss Puddleduck in pink shawl and hat
Who walked with a waddle - oh! Just fancy that!

And then spare a thought for a jolly fat frog,
Jeremy Fisher by name,
Who fished all day long and sat on a log -
His days were always the same!

Consider it fully, those bad little kittens,
Ginger and Pickles and Moppet,
Who returned from the wood without any mittens
And their mother told them to 'Hop it!'

Don't forget Chin-Chin and poor Alexander,
The pigs from the tale Pigling Bland.
Then there's Hunca Munca, the Tailor of Gloucester
And all the mice you could fit in your hand.

Imagine no more, all this is true
And I'm sure this person is well-known to you.
Each badger and mouse, rabbit and otter,
Were all brought to you by the great Beatrix Potter!

Nathalie Gale (13)

CLASSIC MOTORBIKE
(Taken from true-life experiences)

Kick-start her engine to get her to run,
Her exhaust pipe fires like a gun,
The body starts to squeal,
As up goes her front wheel,
She's a classic motorbike.

She can feel her heavy load,
As she glides along the road,
As she stops at a red light,
Her engine giving her a fight,
She's a classic motorbike.

Down a hill the engine stalls, landing in a heap,
In the end she gets a lift from a sparkling jeep,
In the junkyard now she sits waiting for her day to come,
She's a classic motorbike,
If only she could run!

Paul Schiernecker

LAUREN

Playful, angelic
bouncing, giggling, waiting
playing outside, devilishly grinning
screaming, cackling, whinging
happy, cheeky
sister.

Stacy Moxey (11)
Beauchamps High School

WINTER

The frost on people's cars,
the dew on the grass,
the snow on the trees,
the ice on the roads,
the steam from your breath,
the coldness of your hands,
the bright red of your nose,

the Christmas prezzies,
the cheerful smiles,
the joy of the carol singers,
the grins on the icy snowmen,
the snowball fights on the street,
the family gatherings,
the New Year celebrations,
that's what I think of winter.

Joanne Fenner (12)
Beauchamps High School

MY SISTER

My sister will ask you what you want for dinner
Like a waitress in a restaurant.

She will study and revise from books
Like a professor in a lab room.

Fiercely she will roar like a lion if you
                        touch her make-up and CDs

Sam Little (11)
Beauchamps High School

I CAN'T WRITE A POEM

I can't write a poem
I can't do it without knowing
I don't have a title
How could I miss something so vital?
Whether which pen I should choose
Red or white, black or blue?

I can't write a poem
I can't do it without knowing
I don't have a rhythm
How could I dance like a dancing gibbon
Whether I should write it long or short
In which way I was taught

I can write a poem
I can do it without knowing
I do believe
How could I not understand
And take this wild spirit underhand

I can write a poem
And get those words off my chest
I can write a poem
And I know how to write it best!

Rebecca Lyon (12)
Beauchamps High School

ROLLER SKATING

Bending, running, spinning fast
On my roller skates
then I foolishly ask if I can
Race with all my mates

Twisting, jumping, twirling round
I think I might have won
If I hadn't taken a sudden fall
And landed on my bum.

Georgia Norman (12)
Beauchamps High School

POEMS

Some people can recite poems
Straight out of their minds,
But I am just not
The imaginative kind!

Some people make
Their lyrics flow,
But my brain is on
A go-slow!

Some people are good
At expressing their feelings,
But I just sit
And stare at the ceiling!

Some people can assemble
Their sentences like puzzles,
But my phrases
Just end up in a muddle.

I wriggle in my sea,
Sigh and tap my pen.
Oh, this is no good
I'll have to start again!

Charlotte Carroll (12)
Beauchamps High School

SCHOOL

We're finally at the school gates.
We ramble in, chatting to our mates.
Asking what lessons everyone's got.
Thinking of the books we've forgot.

We're now in; it's ten to nine.
Teachers say 'No talking in the line.'
We wander in to registration.
Doing our ties with frustration.

First lesson's netball.
No running in the hall.
Spit chewing gum in the bin.
Hand all our homework in.

Lunchtime is over and done.
Drama is next; it's really fun.
Lessons are going really slow,
But now it's three-thirty, so it's time to go.

Shayla Sloane (12)
Beauchamps High School

THE BIRTHDAY POEM

B   is for the *best* day of the year.
I   is for the *invitations* given out.
R   is for *receiving* the wonderful gifts.
T   is for *thinking* 'Don't let this day end.'
H   is for *happiness* when you see all your friends.
D   is for my *delicious* birthday cake.
A   is for *always* enjoying this special day.
Y   is for another *year* gone.

Aimee Bond (11)
Beauchamps High School

BIKE

The first thing I do
When I get home from school
Is go to the shed
And get out my bike!

I climb on the saddle
And pedal off at speed
To the local park
Where there's everything I need.

From berms to table-tops
Step-ups to six-packs.
I try them all
Except sometimes
When I stumble and fall.

James Browne (11)
Beauchamps High School

IF ONLY I COULD TAKE ONE SNOWFLAKE HOME

Snowflakes like insects drifting down . . .
Without a hum they come . . .
Without a hum they go . . .

Snowflakes like insects drifting down . . .

If only I could take one home with me to
            to show my friends in the sun . . .

Just for fun . . .

Just for fun . . .

Kevin Baldwin (12)
Beauchamps High School

LOST

It's quiet
Now
The sky is dark

An hour ago
I heard him bark

From some distance
Near the hill, then everything
Grew
Hushed and still

A wind came
Rippling the grass

I thought
I saw his shadow
Pass

But it turned out to be a breeze making patterns
Of the trees and bushes where the fence post meets

I stand here.

Looking down
The street
Watching
Strange shapes
In the dark

I wait
I listen for his bark.

Natalie Fullbrook (13)
Beauchamps High School

GOAL

The sun was shining on the pitch
The players all came out
The crowd went wild just to see
The ball being kicked about.

The ref's the one from Italy
The one we met before
We played against Argentina
It was a 2-all draw.

In the 18th minute
Germany almost scored a goal
But David Seaman caught it
And blocked it from the hole.

My mum, she made a cup of tea
When the game was at half-time
Either team has yet to score
The ball must cross the line.

Shearer, he has scored a goal
To make the score 1-0
I hope that at the end of the game
We are winning still.

Well, England have just won the match
With Shearer's winning goal
Need to beat Romania
Next time with Paul Scholes.

Beckham did a great job
Campbell and Owen too
We mustn't leave out Ince-y
Next time we'll win by two.

Katie Sparrow (12)
Beauchamps High School

ADRENALIN

As you walk, you pump through my body
I round the corner of the alleyway
It's dark, I'm filled with fear
You make me go hot and cold.

You run round my blood at the speed of light
Pumping fear right through me
As I come to a stop
You suddenly go away
I'm glad it's all over
Till you come back tomorrow.

Ruth Cash (14)
Beauchamps High School

BLUE DAY

A famous arena,
West London it is,
Down the Fulham Road,
A sea of blue, paints the street,
Oceans of people chant together,
Stools line the meandering tarmac river,
Crowds slowly seep from on the street.
The mighty arena, the Acropolis, the Bridge
As the clock strikes three,
The crowd's heroes emerge,
Chelsea, Chelsea, Chelsea!

Marcus Lambert (14)
Beauchamps High School

MY FAVOURITE SUBJECT

Maths is really cool.
It is the best subject at school.
We are learning decimals, to the left and right.
There is something easy in sight.
The calculators are there because we need 'em.
My maths teacher is Mr Beedham.
Next Wednesday we have a test.
This will decide who is the best.
We have maths three times a week
And I would not miss it at its peak.
This is the time to revise our work
We will then get a good mark.

Shane Greenwood (14)
Beauchamps High School

MR CROC

There was a great crocodile
Whose name was Mr Croc.
All day long he would rest by a rock
When the sun went down and the moon came up
Old Mr Croc would come out to sup.
He would eat his fill until he needed an
                                    indigestion pill
Then off he would go, oh so slow
Back to his rock to sleep.
                        Goodbye Mr Croc.

Tom Penny (11)
Beauchamps High School

SCENTS AND SMELLS

Roses smell really sweet,
Much better than smelly feet,
The air really smells,
But no one can tell.

Most of the animals really pong,
And I think that is really wrong,
I like the smell of grass being cut,
But I hate the smell of a pig's hut,
I like the smell of food being cooked,
And I like the smell of brand new books.

The scent of flowers,
Wafts through the towers,
The sweet scent of perfume,
Always lingers in the room.

Charlotte Hollis (11)
Beauchamps High School

LOVE

Love is like a strawberry
It's red just like your heart
It never goes out of fashion
It's sweet while it lasts.

It could be really sour
Or it could be really nice
But then again
You can never be sure
What it's going to be like.

Kirsty Hollis (14)
Beauchamps High School

SEASONS

Winter starts the year,
Children playing snowballs,
Skaters gliding across the frozen ponds,
Snowmen looking down upon us with coal-black eyes.

Spring comes with great relief,
The earth is warmed beneath us,
Flowers start to grow and wonderful scents fill the air.

Summer's sun sets in for good,
The temperature's rising daily,
Finally the end of school comes and everybody
                             goes off on their hols.

Autumn brings the darker days,
Leaf upon leaf falls from the trees,
Hallowe'en and Guy Fawkes bring the thrills and spills
                             and Catherine wheels.

Nichola Bailey (11)
Beauchamps High School

LET'S CELEBRATE!

Best wishes
It's special
Read your cards
Tear open your presents
Hear the singing
Date
A wish
Yeah! Let's party!
Some cake!

Katie Taylor (11)
Beauchamps High School

SEA SHANTY

The ship moved out of the harbour as carefully as could be,
The captain steered the vessel smoothly out to sea.
The sailors were experienced and used to life away,
They had chosen to be sailors and not farmers making hay.
The cabin boy prepared his bunk, he knew what was in store;
This wasn't his first voyage, he'd been sailing twice before.
The journey was a long one, it lasted for six weeks
Many islands they had searched, with treasure for to seek.

The time had come for their return, they loaded up the hold.
Their plundering was successful, with silver, bronze and gold;
But on the return voyage, the storms began to blow.
The ship turned round in circles and didn't know where to go.
The captain lost control and the ship began to sink;
The treasure and the crew were all washed into the brink.
So what became of them all?
No one will ever know, but the gold upon the seabed will
                              stay locked up and glow!

Sean Clark (11)
Beauchamps High School

A CHEETAH

Aggressive, evil
Speedy, fast, quick
Swooping through the grass
Ripping, tearing, quick
Quick and good
Prey.

Michael Ridge (11)
Beauchamps High School

THE WHITE RABBIT

The white rabbit that sits above my pencil,
How I wish it was real,
Oh I wish I could hold it in my arms,
I could sit and watch it play all day,
I wish I could talk to it when I get lonely,
It would be the perfect friend for me,
I could even give it a name,
Oh how I wish it was real!
I could even get a bowl with its name on it,
It could have its own home in my back garden,
It would always be there when I get home,
It would be so pleased to see me, it would run up
                                    and down its cage,
I would always know it was pleased to see me as it
                would be smiling at me in its own way.

If only wishes could come true!

Kayleigh Parrish-King (14)
Beauchamps High School

MY BEST FRIENDS

My best friend is Hal because she is so cool,
But Stacey is so brill because she is so tall.

My next best friend is Kirsty because she is so mad,
And I like Josephine because she's never sad.

I cannot choose a best friend because they're all too nice
But millions and millions of good friends are what I call Paradise!

Emily Kenny (11)
Beauchamps High School

HORSES

My horse!
Jumping over jumps
Galloping over bumps
Trotting in the wind
First place she wins!

Too hot to handle
Palomino randle
Golden mane
She has no shame.

In her royal red
Her hoof does tread
Another winning
Just like the beginning!

Shining bright
Within her right
Vera holds the night

Sam Pheby (13)
Beauchamps High School

MY CAT HARRY

I have a cat called Harry
who gets into lots of fights.
That's because he's out every night.
He's got big, green eyes, and he's black and white.
He moans when he wants to be fed,
and he sleeps on my bed.
That's my cat Harry.

Joanna McLean (11)
Beauchamps High School

SNOWFLAKES!

Snowflakes fell on my face,
It felt like cold hands.
It covered the whole place,
And you couldn't see one bit of land.

All of the snowflakes fell on my hair,
They were like crystals shining very bright.
In the distance I saw some polar bears,
My sister had a fright!

The bears were eating fish,
They thought it looked nice.
This was always my wish,
To go skating on the ice.

We went skating which was fun,
I thought it was all a dream.
We all fell over, and landed on our bum,
So I went home with my sister and had
                        some custard and cream!

Hazel Cole (14)
Beauchamps High School

ALONE

They hide in darkness, alone,
afraid of change and afraid of God!
They must get so lonely, no soul,
no feelings, no remorse, no friends,
no memories, no reason for existence
No life . . . *vampires!*

James Trott (13)
Beauchamps High School

MY CAT

Fearlessly
She leaps out to catch her prey
Like a vicious terrifying
Lion.

Wildly
She rips her prey in half
Like an angry
Cheetah.

Viciously
She drags and hides her prey
Like a dangerous
Bear.

Jemma Balloo (11)
Beauchamps High School

CARS

Cars . . .

Big ones, small ones, short ones, tall ones,
3-seater, 4-seater, 7-seater, 50-seater,
2-door, 3-door, 4-door, 5-door.
Fiat, Ford, Vauxhall, Chrysler, Ferrari, Porsche.

Cars, cars, so many cars, but which one to pick,
that's the trick.

Keke Sheard (13)
Beauchamps High School

POEMS

I can't write poems
Everybody knows it
But I can try and there's
No harm in it.

All you can do is have a go,
That's what I believe!
If you get it wrong that's what
You can try and achieve.

When you eventually get it right,
You will know that you've turned on a light.
When I say 'turn on a light' I mean inside you.
Now when you get nervous in English
It won't be because of poetry it will
be when I say . . . 'Boo!'

Amy Markham (11)
Beauchamps High School

ENGLISH

E   is for *expressive*
N   is for *no* paragraphs
G   is for being *good* in lessons
L   is for *listening*
I   is for *interesting*
S   is for *sentences*
H   is for *hyphens.*

Dean Bishop (13)
Beauchamps High School

MY MAD PONY

I look ahead and hope for a clear round,
My pony takes off feet firmly off the ground.
I jump the double with no trouble
Then comes the next jump
We land with a thump
We canter on getting faster and faster
I know that this is going to be a disaster
My horse is uncontrollable now
I think, am going to stay on and how?
I know in my head I've got no chance of winning,
This happens every time
I thought my pony was getting better by loads,
But obviously not because
I wouldn't have a bad back or sore toes,
Everyone tells me my fall wasn't too bad,
But I just think you're lucky
You're pony ain't mad.

Kayleigh Branson (13)
Beauchamps High School

BIRTHDAY

B   irthdays come every year,
I   t's when you have no worries or fear!
R   ing your friends and invite them round,
T   ime for a new outfit to be found!
H   urry up, it's nearly time,
D   anielle's the first to arrive!
A   t half-past ten they have all gone home.
Y   es, that's the end of my little poem!

Lauren Pigg (14)
Beauchamps High School

THE TUNNEL OF DEATH

Through the ice-cold
tunnel I walk,
step by step, shivering,
able to see my own breath,
tiptoeing through the
pitch-black water,
my feet freezing into icebergs,
not knowing what to expect!
Staring forward with those bloodshot eyes,
not daring to turn around,
screaming inside but can't speak a word,
just want to escape!
My mind just tells me to turn back,
but I'm too afraid!

Stephanie Meszaros (12)
Beauchamps High School

THE WISE OLD OWL

The old owl sits in its rotting tree
Prowling for his next victim of prey
He hoots in the night sky
Spreading his wings as he flies away
In search of his next victim of prey
His wings shine in the moonlit sky
as he gets further away
He's now spotted his prey
He plummets to the ground
With a great swooping sound.
Did he get it, or did it get away?

Andrew Burns (14)
Beauchamps High School

LION

Lion,
Ferocious, deadly
Stalks, sprints, commands
King of the jungle
Powerful, bold
Fierce.

Samantha Anthony (12)
Beauchamps High School

WHAT IS ORANGE?

What is orange?
Is it a colour that represents hot,
Which you can paint your car or paint your yacht?
Does it mean get ready on a traffic light,
Or is it for a firework which goes out of sight?
It's the colour of lava that is spewed out of a volcano,
But it's my favourite colour, that's all I know.

Craig Budgen (13)
Beauchamps High School

BLUE SHEEP

Blue sheep jump high
Blue sheep can fly
Blue sheep are cool
Blue sheep wear wool
Blue sheep are seen
When I shut my eyes and dream.

Kate North (13)
Beauchamps High School

ENGLAND

E agerly waiting fans
N oisily cheering on the players
G reat goals being scored
L ights beaming down on the pitch
A ngry at the referee
N early getting sent off
D ynamic daring England team.

Sarah Greenwood (11)
Beauchamps High School

SHARK

S wimming in the ocean deep
H ere we have a shark
A mongst fish, a predator
R arely do they sleep
K ing of the sea.

Mark Stitson (11)
Beauchamps High School

THE GOALIE

G is for gloves that help me to catch
O is for offside signalled during the match
A is for the attackers who make me save
L is for linesman, whose flag he does wave
I is for intercepting the highest cross that you've seen
E is for eleven players in my team.

Robert Forster (11)
Beauchamps High School

THE CRAVING

I sat there in darkness, all alone,
I could hardly breathe.
All I could think of was the fact I needed them,
The thing I couldn't live without,
The thing I needed most in my life,
The thing everyone was talking about,
But I could never get it,
I was so upset I could cry forever.

If I could get that thing I wanted,
I would be happy for the rest of my life.
But I forgot all about everyone around me,
I even stopped loving people I loved most before,
But it still didn't stop me taking them,
Oh I wish I hadn't started,
And I wish I never let my friends talk me into it,
But what can I do about it now? (nothing.)

I must admit my life was super without them,
Now look at me, I'm a mess,
Now my life is hell,
Oh how I badly need them,
I really wish I could have what I wanted,
I could remember thinking just about them,
What I had wanted for a long time.
There was only one way to get them . . .
By stealing things for them,

Lisa Clement (14)
Beauchamps High School

PEOPLE

People, people everywhere
Who they are I don't care
Different types of skin wherever I might look
Different type of jobs
Maybe a doctor, teacher or a cook
People with eyes brown, green or blue
Mixed up colours, hazelnut too.

Various religions we all have them
Muslim, Christian, Jewish and Hinduism
Beliefs which you would like to choose
There's many more you cannot lose.

People might live in a house or a flat
But people on the streets make do with a mat.
Do people live in peace?
Do people live in fear?
There might be a war
Will it be near?

Some people rich, some people poor
Some people in the middle, they'll not be sure
Some people selfish, they'll just want more.

A different accent a different way
This is how we are from day to day
Into the world these people came
Individual people, there are no two the same.

Deborah Leworthy (12)
Beauchamps High School

MY BROTHER

B   oring brother!
R   ude brother!
O   utspoken brother!
T   errible brother!
H   orrible brother!
E   njoys fighting brother!
R   eally annoying brother!

Danny Lockley (12)
Beauchamps High School

HUNTING

Declines the sun
as the moon intrudes,
in this unfamiliar place,
under the mask of the dark,
the unspoken observe the unwary
and wait for the time . . .

Joseph Fay (15)
Beauchamps High School

RABBIT

R   unning, hopping, bouncing bunny
A   nxiously going in circles around the garden
B   unnies are cuddly
B   ut big and plump too
I   t nibbles anything
T   hat goes for your finger too.

Brittany Tovey (11)
Beauchamps High School

WHY?

On a day like any other day,
A sadness swept the world,
When people went about their way,
A disaster struck America today.

Why is there anger?
Why is there pain?
Do any people have any shame?
Lives are taken,
Lives are lost,
Lives are supposed to be lived,
Not at a cost.

When so many people lost their lives,
Husband, children, mums and wives,
When two towers fell,
The dust, the smoke,
The awful smell,
The tears that have been shed,
May this now put peace in people's heads?

Why is there terror?
Why is there pain?
This appears throughout the year,
But among the bad,
The wrong and the cruel,
There is good upon us all.

For all the families who now have to suffer,
Let's all hope we can comfort each other.
The world is behind you all the way
God bless America each and every day.

Katie Bloomfield (14)
Beauchamps High School

A TIGER'S DAY

T   hirsty in the hot desert
I   dle animals in the grass
G   ush past for the nearest food
E   legant as the silent sea
R   aging like the wind.

Gemma Maycey (11)
Beauchamps High School

TIMETABLE

On Monday I have assembly, I don't think it's great.
On Tuesday I have RE right before break.
On Wednesday, we have nice things like music and art.
On Thursday we have drama, it's good for the heart.
On Friday we have ICT, it is great fun
Because Friday is the last day, let the weekend come!

Bobby Ellis (11)
Beauchamps High School

SNAKE

S   lithers stealthily, no one sees him
N   ever looks away
A   ble to speed across the land
K   eeps still till he strikes
E   dging ever closer.

Luke Essam (11)
Beauchamps High School

MY SISTER

S illy sister
I impulsive sister
S ulking sister
T errible sister
E njoys fighting sister
R ude sister.

My sister!

Scott Collins (11)
Beauchamps High School

TIGER

Stripes shining, coat conspicuous
Fearsome fangs, rapid rate, cutting claws
More haste, less speed
Fearsome fangs, rapid rate, cutting claws
Stripes shining, coat conspicuous.

Sharon Wilton (11)
Beauchamps High School

SCHOOL

S chool bus is coming
C lock says eight
H ope I'm ready
O r I will be late
O nly just made it
L ast one at the gate.

Jay Fedelmesi (11)
Beauchamps High School

I Don't Get It

I've got a form tutor called Mr Clown,
but why do I need a clown to teach a form?
When do I have to fill it in anyway?
Next I've got English, but what's the point in that?
I'm already English!
My brother said I would need a locker,
but I get claustrophobic, and how do I get in that?
Who's Mrs Bony Face?
A bag of bones isn't gonna make a good teacher!
I'm learning woodwork in a week of two,
I didn't know wood could work
or could woodwork?
Got gym next, wonder what he's like!

Daniel Lambert (11)
Beauchamps High School

Smelliest

S   ocks are very pongy but
M   uch better than
E   ggs that are rotten.
L   ots of people like the smell of
L   ong-stemmed flowers.
I   like the
E   arly morning frost that is as
S   weet as candyfloss
T   ogether with snow.

Alexandra Buckingham (11)
Beauchamps High School

THE EMBARRASSMENT

Walking down the path,
See a woman trying to park,
Oh no, off comes her bumper,
Oh my God, it's my mother,
I cross the road and pretend not to know her,
She calls across for some help,
I said 'You're having a laugh, I don't know ya,'
'But I'm your mother,
I've just got back from picking up your brother,
So get back here before I tell your father.'
I look around, curtains twitching,
Next door's looking our her kitchen,
Tutting and shaking her head,
She turns to tell her husband Fred!

Shelley Sweet (13)
Beauchamps High School

BUTTERFLY

B   eautiful wings shining bright
U   nbelievably smart and a wonderful sight
T   ransformed from a caterpillar
T   o a lovely butterfly
E   verybody loves them and I know why
R   arely you see them around, they fly
F   luttering about the bright, blue sky
L   earning to be friends with everyone in sight
Y   ou should be lucky because you have a friend for life.

Sheena Alexander (11)
Beauchamps High School

LITTLE ANGEL

Loving, caring
I am an angel
Topsy
Turvey
Like little lambs
Elegant little darlings

Amber eyes
Nice blonde hair
Giant wings
Little tiny feet
Excellent timing
Angels!

Gemma Louise Wood (13)
Beauchamps High School

CHINCHILLA

C   autiously the chinchilla moves around the house.
H   appily the chinchilla munches on its food.
I   mpersonating a statue.
N   early having a munch on an apple while no one's looking
C   almly the chinchilla jumps off the table.
H   oping the giants forget he's out,
I   f the giants forget he's out, he can stay out forever.
L   uckily the chinchilla dodges the hands of the giants.
L   ooking at the monsters through the door that are called cats.
A   fter a couple of hours the chinchilla makes its way to the cage.

Liam Roper-Browning (11)
Beauchamps High School

THE COSMOS

Beyond the clouds and the sky
there is a void of space
where things drift by and by.

There are stars all of which are gleaming light
but some will explode with frightening might.

Planets are made of a rocky mass
others are just simply gas.

Asteroids fly and then they crash
watch out for a comet
you'll miss it in a flash.

Things are moving at an incredible pace
in this strange world we call space.

John Leworthy (14)
Beauchamps High School

DOLPHINS

D   arkest, deepest sea,
O   ceans clear and free,
L   et me wish I could be,
P   laying with them in the sea.
H   eavenly creatures from God's hands,
I   dentified around the land,
N   ever to be hurt, but free,
S   wimming around for all eternity.

Kayleigh Baines (11)
Beauchamps High School

THINGS THAT GO BUMP IN THE NIGHT!

It's nearly midnight
I am in my bed cosy and tight
I close my eyes to go to sleep
But the ghosts are making
The floorboards creak.

I think there's a ghost
Knocking at my door
But not only one
There's lots more.

In the bushes
I can hear rustling
But I am not sure
If it's my mum and dad fussing!

Laura Warton (12)
Beauchamps High School

MY WORLD

I like to sit and read a book,
out in the kitchen I like to cook.
Running about is just so good,
I'd love to fly, I wish I could.
I like to slouch and watch TV
and enjoy putting tons of sugar in my tea.
It's lovely watching my rabbit hop about
and the noise of my guinea pig squeal and shout.
But the worst thing of all is going to bed,
I've had enough, it's going to my head!

Chloe Still (11)
Beauchamps High School

THE BEST DAD

My dad Gary is a real good bloke,
His chest is really hairy,
Mum says he's a gentle giant,
But we think that he's scary.

He's got no hair
And the odd spot
And a very deep voice to match.
But he's my favourite person
And Mum says 'Wow, what a good catch.'

Good old Gary, he's the best,
With his wrinkly, hairy chest,
Spots and pimples, getting bald,
He's the nicest dad of them all.

Katie White (13)
Beauchamps High School

FIRST DAY OF SCHOOL

It's my first day of school
How uncool!
I'm in school, I feel great
But all my friends are in a state!
My teacher's great and really kind,
But as we talk, time flies by.
As the bell rings, everyone rushes home
But as I leave, I go quite slow
It's my first day at school
How uncool.

Charlotte Stanners (11)
Beauchamps High School

RABBITS

Rabbits here
Rabbits there
Little rabbits
Everywhere

Hopping here
Hopping there
Grazing in the
Sunny air

Autumn comes
Then winter snow
Bye bye bunnies
Time to go.

Krystina Hopkins (11)
Beauchamps High School

I LIKE TO THROW LOTS OF THINGS

I like to throw lots of things,
Discus, shot and javelins.
I throw javelins on a Monday night.
I'm the youngest there, so it's a bit of a fright,
I run down the runway really fast
I let go of the javelin
With a big, big blast
It flies through the air like an arrow in flight
If it lands point first then I've done it all right.

Thomas Clayton (11)
Beauchamps High School

LITTLE RACING CAR

Little racing car
Waiting at the start
Little racing car
Looking really smart
All the other cars said go
But little racing car said no!
Little racing car
All in a muddle
Little racing car
Drove through a puddle
Little racing car
Took a hit
Little racing car
In the pit
Little racing car
Getting a repair
Little racing car
Said hurry up no time to spare!
Little racing car
Back in the race
Little racing car
Back on the chase!
Little racing car
Gets a speed burst
Little racing car
Up to first!
Little racing car
Speeding round the track
Little racing car
Takes the chequered flag!

Chris Mizen (11)
Beauchamps High School

AGE

As free as a bird I was at one
and only attached and fed by my mum.

When I was two and began to walk
I would look all around and watch like a hawk.

When I was small, in fact only three
my dad looked tall, as tall as a tree.

Between four and six I started school
it worried me not, I was like a cucumber, so cool.

Between 7 and 11 my parents had hope
that I would toughen up soon, as tough as old rope.

And now I am twelve and my poem is done
well, for this year at least, until the next one!

Steve Gibson (12)
Beauchamps High School

FOOTBALL

F   ab football, knocking the ball around well,
O   h, I think we're playing at The Dell,
O   i you! I'm in a space,
T   homson just got a boot in his face,
B   ad ball, it should have been here,
A   lright, I'll give you a smash round the ear,
L   ucky ball in the back of the net,
L   ovely ball by Poyet.

Tom De'ath (11)
Beauchamps High School

MY BEST FRIEND

I have a best friend, her name is Holly,
Most of the time she's extremely jolly.
She has a kid sister, we call her B,
B's best friend is called Shelly.

Holly has lots of animals, 15 in all,
A dog, 4 rats, 3 rabbits and guinea pigs small.
I play out with Holly all the time,
We run about and make up rhymes.

Holly's my best friend as you can see,
We always have fun and giggle with glee.
We're always together whatever the weather,
We will be best friends forever and ever.

Emma Pepperell (12)
Beauchamps High School

PHONE BILL

On Monday I rang Sammy, Sarah and Kate,
On Tuesday I rang Emily, she's a very good mate,
On Wednesday I rang Shelley, she has chickenpox,
On Thursday I rang Carol, she's a chatterbox,
On Friday I rang Morgan, we'd talk all day,
On Saturday I rang Amy, and I had nothing to say,
On Sunday the phone bill was posted through our door,
I started to read it for I was curious,
My mum did the same but she was furious!

Kirsty Tremayne (11)
Beauchamps High School

DANCING

Dancing keeps me fit
But a lot of money for the kit.
The dancers' moves are very quick
Lucky for me I'm pretty slick.
We do splits, we do kicks
It doesn't matter who she picks
I am there every night
And I try with all my might.

Clare French (13)
Beauchamps High School

THE SUMMER

S ummer is warm, summer is light.
U p in the sky you can see all night,
M any stars, so small but bright,
M ust it be that the sun is a star at night?
E veryone is being told not to laugh and not to talk,
R ight before the midnight walk.

Elizabeth Graham-Older (11)
Beauchamps High School

PALOMINO

Palomino,
Glamorous, majestic
Galloping, rearing, cantering
Shining, shimmering, glossy body
Jumping, showing, racing
Outstanding, inspiring
Golden.

Josephine Bourner (11)
Beauchamps High School

MY WOOLLY JUMPER

I live in Kuala Lumpur
I have a woolly jumper
And if that girl speaks again
I'll thump her.

Christopher Denny (11)
Beauchamps High School

RUGBY

I like rugby,
I like to shout and run,
We all get together in the middle for a rugby scrum.
The ball gets thrown on the floor, we're pulled to and fro,
One of the players gets the ball, then, off he goes.
We chase him up the field and shout, 'Go, go, go.'
Did he make it to the line?
That I just don't know.
I've been knocked to the floor, I've got mud in my eyes,
Oh well, I don't know if our team will ever score any tries.

Bradley Jarvis (11)
Beauchamps High School

BIRD

B   irds soar across the sky
I   nto eaves and trees
R   esting briefly once in a while
D   ozing in the breeze.

Stephanie Morgan (12)
Beauchamps High School

TV MADNESS!

There's one thing I'd like to know,
How they broadcast each show!

There are the shows that are mind benders,
Just like good old Eastenders!

And then there's programmes like Cold Feet
And Friends and Simpsons and Coronation Street.

There's loads more programmes, that make you laugh,
Or blow a fuse,
Even one's that make you cry, or serious like the news!

There's just too many programmes, you can't watch them all,
You've got to love your TV. It's really cool!

Lauren Orton (11)
Beauchamps High School

A DOG'S DAY

I saw a dog climb a tree
it sat there looking down at me.

At first I thought what a lark
until the dog began to bark.

I wondered what it was playing at
until I saw it had chased a cat.

I bet it sat there all night and day
until the rain fell the following day.

Aaron Pitts (11)
Beauchamps High School

MONSTERS UNDER MY BED

When it's time to go to sleep,
I go upstairs to do my teeth.
My mum comes in to say goodnight,
And then I have a great big fright.
My mum has gone, she's shut the door,
I see a shadow on the floor.
I see a hand under my bed,
'I'm gonna eat you,' the monster said.
I made a break for the door,
But then he slid along the floor.
He stopped me from getting to my mum,
So I kicked him in the bum.
He got really angry, what could I do?
So he grabbed my leg and pulled it too.
Things couldn't be as strange as they seem,
Then I woke up, it was a dream.

Danielle Fazekas (12)
Beauchamps High School

THE LA-LA MONSTER

The La-La monster is friendly
He is also tall and fat
His eyes are green and sparkly
Just like my neighbour's cat
He tries to scare my friends away
But they just think he's funny
They laugh at him and make him cry
Then he says 'Where's my mummy?'

Mark Hopkins (13)
Beauchamps High School

GHOSTS AND GHOULS

It's midnight,
I'm in bed,
I'm feeling cosy,
I heard a noise,
I thought it was ghosts slamming doors,
But it was only the thunder outside.
It's 1 o'clock,
I'm in bed,
I'm feeling uncomfortable,
I heard a noise,
I thought it was blood dripping,
But it was only the tap running.
It's 2 o'clock,
I'm on the floor,
I'm feeling very scared,
I heard a noise,
I thought it was ghosts coming up the stairs,
But it was only Mum opening the door.
It's 3 o'clock,
I'm in bed,
I'm asleep,
It's silent,
That's better.
'Night.

Robert Dennis (12)
Beauchamps High School

LOVE

Love is sweet, love is kind
    for some it takes a bit longer to find
the perfect someone who really loves you
    the one who is your dream come true

No matter if it's not the right one
   just carry on and keep having fun!
Don't drive yourself around the bend
   you always meet one in the end.

Faye Rider (14)
Beauchamps High School

MY FAVOURITE PLACE

In the middle of a wood
The tree stands big and bold
Then all alone on the highest branch
Lies my favourite place.

The walls are jagged and rough
The floor cold and smooth
The window made of plastic
But it's still my favourite place.

The most spectacular scenery is out of the window
For me to gaze at all day
It may be muddy and dirty
But it's only a house for me.

The long rope ladder
Hanging wildly like a snake
The door made from a cardboard box
But it's only my hideaway.

From my bedroom window
I can see a wood
Then way up high in the tallest tree
Lies my favourite place.

Mitchell Brooks (12)
Beauchamps High School

MY BROTHER

I have a brother,
an annoying brother.
He beats me up,
it hurts so much.
He gets me in trouble,
then I get grounded.
He's so horrible to me,
he's meant to be my brother.
When he has a temper,
he takes it out on me.
I hate him so much,
but I know really I love him inside.

Kayleigh Anderson (13)
Beauchamps High School

WINNING

Football is a brilliant thing
Especially when you're winning
When we score I scream and shout
And dance and skip and run about.

When we win the biggest prize
I look and see the crowd all rise
I love it when the crowd go mad
All the team are very glad.

We won, we won in super style
This won't sink in for quite a while.

Aaron Omand (13)
Beauchamps High School

GHOSTS

This is a poem about ghosts.
Hi, I am Troy, this is your host.
Are they there while you're sleeping?
Under the covers are you peeping?
Creaking floorboards, what could it be?
Checking the time, it's half-past three.
Lying there, shall I get out
To see what is really about?
I get up and open the door
I see a shadow on the floor.
I look around the narrow corner
The misty thing is getting taller.
I close my eyes and wait and see
A little mouse is looking at me.

Troy Mainstone (12)
Beauchamps High School

SISTERS

They will be there for you
whatever you may do
Whether they're older than you
or younger than you
They're the best
though you may not think it
They may stress you out
and give you a fit
So all in all sisters will be with you
till the end.

Kerry Hammond (13)
Beauchamps High School

ALL CHANGE

At the moment I am in Year 6, Great Berry Primary.
In six weeks' time I will be in Year 7, Secondary Beauchamps.
Beauchamps.
What do you do?
Do you have to be a champ to get into the school?
Do you get expelled if you are not one?
The teachers at Great Berry say we will become students.
What's a student?
Do you have to eat stew and obtain a dent in your head?
I don't know.

The lunch place is a hall at Great Berry.
they call it a cafeteria at Beauchamps.
What's that?
I have only ever heard of a cafeteria in The Simpsons.
Does that mean that Beauchamps is an American school?
I won't know what to do.
Everything is all change.

David Westall (11)
Beauchamps High School

A CAT

I pluck with needle-like claws
at my prey, a bird.
Ripping and tearing at the soft flesh
I'm hungry!

I purr poetically
Like the warm humming of the radiator
I'm warm!

Samantha Root (12)
Beauchamps High School

FEAR

Falling to the dark underworld,
Water surrounding, everywhere you look,
The silence, stinging your eyes,
Breathless, drags life under.

The scramble up to the surface,
Is a matter of life or death,
But the huge, blue water demon,
Will not let anyone rest.

The smash as your body hits the water,
The chance of survival is low,
As the surface begins to disappear,
The oxygen bubbles get smaller.

There is no chance of living,
As the blue water demon still bites,
Your body begins to get weaker,
As you know you have lost the fight.

Carla-Jane Brooks (14)
Beauchamps High School

CORNBE GOES TO SCHOOL

It's time for school
I knock for Paul
It's quarter to nine
We're just in time
We go to break
Let's buy a cake
This bit's cool
End of school.

Craig Smith (13)
Beauchamps High School

MY DOGS

They run around all day
They really like to play
They wind me up sometimes
They bark and stare
With their deep, dark eyes
Do you know what they're thinking?
They're always full of surprise
With envy in their eyes
Secrets and surprise
They cry when they don't get their way
They're always in despair
They think we do not care
They always want food
And long walks everywhere
They love it in the sun
They're always having fun
They love to frighten birds
They smell the scent of foxes in the air.

Melissa Baldwin (13)
Beauchamps High School

FOOTBALL

F   antastic
O   ffside
O   ver the top
T   eam spirit
B   one crunching tackles
A   gonising
L   ovable
L   aughable.

Martin Lawrence (13)
Beauchamps High School

The Roller Coaster

As I step in the carriage
The safety bar comes down
People have looks on their faces
Some with a frown.

I slowly crawl up the top
Hanging from a great big drop
All of a sudden I begin to fall
Swirling, turning, looping, I think it's cool.

People screaming with fear
Some even with a tear
At this point
People want to get off!

Whooshing high and low
But I now begin to slow
Back where we started
That's the story of the roller coaster.

Louise Black (12)
Beauchamps High School

My Poem

Just think of every
Pleasant thing
You'd like to do today,
And then you'll know
The wishes
That this greeting brings
Your way!
Happy birthday!

Martin Vidgeon (12)
Beauchamps High School

UNITED

When people die close to you a part of your heart burns to ashes
Being hijacked, where people die, when the plane they are on crashes
It makes me wonder if God exists, where is he now, does he even care?
About the people who died in those hijacked planes and having people
dare to risk their lives too
We do wonder why a person would kill thousands of innocent people
and who he was trying to fool
Because, boy he isn't cool
To think he would get away with murder, doesn't show he's brave
It shows he is a coward and should be put in an open grave
And rot in hell
When you shed a tear
You feel for the people who fear
They have lost the love of their lives
And feel a thousand knives
Cutting your life into pieces
Leaving no creases
Of life to spare
It is always there
As you want to but can't rewrite the words of God
Heroes saving people and bringing them to safety risking
their own lives
And people leaping out of windows into deadly dives
Shouts and screams to be heard from miles
Even raising the temperature for sundials
England and America will always stay a unity
As at least we have some dignity
The trading towers and Pentagon were a big part of America
They were and always will be in our memories forever
It's more than I can say for Bin Laden.

Laura Bryan (13)
Beauchamps High School

ALL CHANGE

Today, my last day at junior school.
In six weeks I will be a stewdent.
Does that mean they feed us stew?
Yuck! I hate stew!

I am going to Beauchamps.
I hope I don't have to be a champion.
I'm not much good at sport.

Six weeks over, now I'm here.
This place is huge!
I've got to find C1.
Is this my room number?
Do the teachers come to us?

They tell us to go to the hall.
It's great compared to Wickford Juniors.
No more cold, hard floors!
Lovely comfy chairs
All in rows!
So many people!

I'm off to meet my tudor,
I'm sure when we did tudors
They said they were all dead.
God, it might be Henry VIII.
Yeah! That would be cool!
Unless he chops my head off!

We feed the vending machines and they give us food.
Do these robots eat coins I wonder?
Everything is all change.

Shelley Manning (11)
Beauchamps High School

FRIENDS

Friends are people you can play with.
Friends are people you should be with.
Friends are people you can trust.
Friends are people who keep in touch.

Friends are people who are kind.
Friends are people who you can find.
Friends are people who stand by your side.

Friends are people who never lie.
Friends are people who stick together.
Friends should be friends forever.

Kirstie Phillips (12)
Beauchamps High School

SMELLY FEET

My family think my feet smell,
But I don't think they do.
I put clean socks on every day,
Even if I don't have to.
They say my feet smell cheesy,
But I think they smell nice.
They always say I should spray my feet
With a bit of Old Spice.
My family have tried everything,
To stop my smelly feet.
They even think my feet smell
Like really mouldy meat.

Alex Sparks (11)
Beauchamps High School

MY ROOM AT NIGHT

Every night when I lie in bed,
Spooky thoughts run through my head.

Trees out my window make a scary shape,
While the monster under my bed tries to escape.

Outside my door I hear my parents chatter,
And the leaves on the trees make a noisy clatter.

Then all of a sudden I hear a knock at the door,
Could it be the monsters on the floor?

Then my eyes go blurry, then go blank,
I've fallen asleep and will not wake!
Those monsters are a piece of cake!

Anna Sampson (11)
Beauchamps High School

DOLPHINS

Dolphins swim the seas wild,
splendid and free.
Dolphins like company,
I hope they like me!
I jump in the sea
and up they come to me.
We swim for a while
then we go our own way.
I shall remember forever
the day they swam with me!

Joanna Ramsay (12)
Beauchamps High School

LITTLE BROTHER

Little brother short and sweet,
Is that smell your smelly feet?
You may be mean, but I'm not keen,
To play your silly games.
You call me names, which isn't fun,
You shoot me with your water gun.
But little bro I love you so,
No matter what you do.

Jemma Donnelly (13)
Beauchamps High School

DOLPHINS

Dolphins swimming in the sea,
They come up and jump with glee.
Swimming around in a show,
Jumping through hoops high and low.
These friendly mammals,
Are certainly not camels.
They are fast and sleek,
And can almost speak.
How intelligent they can be,
As they swim brightly in the sea.

Keely Murnane (12)
Beauchamps High School

GROTBAG SCHOOL

Grotbag School is a terrible place,
You should see the headmaster's face,
He has a ring through his nose,
With a chain that hangs to his toes.

The teachers look like witches, with pimples on their nose,
Warts and ugly blotches, that stick out like thorns on a rose.
The pupils at Grotbag School write more on the walls than paper,
They have snotty noses, that drip like hoses that cause a horrid vapour.

Joe Mullett (11)
Beauchamps High School

I Wish

I wish I could go to space,
But I'm in my room with a sad face,
Thinking that I'm on the moon,
But I'm sitting on my bed in my room,
Walking on the moon from one side to another,
But I'm only under my cover,
Looking out my window I wish I was there,
Everyone knows life isn't fair.

Jazele Parys (12)
Beauchamps High School

Autumn

Summer is ending,
Autumn is near.
Trees shed leaves at this time of year.
Acorns and conkers fall on the ground,
Lying around in heaps and mounds.
Days grow short, damp and dark,
Not the weather for fun in the park.
Autumn, autumn, please pass quick,
I can't wait for Father Nick!

Sophie Donn (12)
Beauchamps High School

MY LIFE

My family is sweet and neat,
They all sit down to rest their feet.

My sisters are rude when they eat their food,
When Dad's in the kitchen, he's a real cool dude.

My rabbits are fluffy, all white and puffy,
They dig big holes which makes them look scruffy.

My bedroom is cool, it has a green stool,
But it doesn't have anywhere for me to play pool.

My house is quite nice, it doesn't have mice,
It's warm and cosy, not cold as ice.
                    I like my life!

Claire Campbell (11)
Beauchamps High School

WINTER

In the winter when it's very cold,
Everyone is miserable, especially the old.
Throwing snowballs at everyone,
Be careful, you're not one.

Scarves, hats and very warm coats,
Without wearing these it gives you a sore throat.
Wrap up warm to avoid a cold,
You should be grateful that you're not old.
So much fun can be gained
In the snow, but not the rain.

Krystal Purcell (12)
Beauchamps High School

MY CAT

My cat is a lovely cat.
He likes playing a lot.
He sleeps on my bed cuddles up with my toys.
He likes going next-door to explore.
He likes the fishpond sometimes he falls in.
He likes catching rats, mice, shrews, birds and insects.
He does fight with other cats.
When he wants feeding he will miaow.
He'll eat ham, turkey and chicken.
He'll play with a ping-pong ball and his string.
He will pounce a lot.
He likes it when you have a box or a carrier bag,
as he will get in it.
My cat is a lovely cat.

Sarah Wallis (11)
Beauchamps High School

FOG

It creeps upon you silently,
Rolling across the ground,
Who knows what lurks within
This hovering mass of the unknown.

It wraps its cold, clammy arms around you,
Making you shiver within
Its shifting embrace.
The fog knows no boundaries
When it creeps across the ground.

Siobain Kirwan (11)
Beauchamps High School

WAR

War, devastating,
Windows shattering,
Wood embers glowing,
Fire engines whizzing around
And putting out blazing fires.
Then I hear the cries of children,
That cover me like a woolly blanket.
War sirens buzzing continuously,
Bang! Bang! The bombs were getting closer.
Bang! One landed right by me
And with that the light fell from my eyes.
I was dead.

Robert Burgess (11)
Beauchamps High School

MY SCHOOL BEAUCHAMPS

B   eauchamps is my school
E   veryone will agree
A   ll the staff are fine
U   niforms are black and white
C   hildren say 'Ha, ha'
H   ere comes the Head
A   nd 'Mind your manners'
M   y mum always said
P   lease and thank you will go far
S   o keep going to school
      and have the time of your life.

Samantha Beeson (11)
Beauchamps High School

THE TV

T ellies make a lot of noise
E verlasting fun
L aughter, sadness, action and romance
E specially on BBC1
V arieties of game shows
I t'll make you laugh and cry
S ome are really embarrassing
I t makes you want to die
O ver on ITV
N ever forget about
            All the fantastic movies
            That make you wanna shout.

Lauren Peckham (11)
Beauchamps High School

CHELSEA V LIVERPOOL

F licking the mud off my boots
O wen said, 'We will beat you'
O n the way to my position
T urn around and see the England manager
B est chance I will ever have
A shot from long distance
L obbed the keeper and it went in. Goal!
L ying on the grass celebrating
E ngland manager approaches
R equired for the World Cup 2002
S uddenly I wake up!

David Huzzey (11)
Beauchamps High School

ALL CHANGE

It's my first day at Beauchamps,
And I'm waiting for the bus.
Oh, here it comes now.

The bus has just arrived.
Hey, I'm outside a big office building now.
So where is my school?
Hey, wait a minute! The gate says 'Beauchamps' on.
Well, they did say we needed a compass.
And where are the police? They said we need to sign a policy.
Oh look, a sign. It says, 'Stewards this way'.
Stewards? Like plane stewards?
That must be why we are wearing these funny suits.
That's weird. We used to be called pupils, like the pupils in your eyes.
Oh, it's the bell. I'm going to my first period of the day now.
One is with my tudor. Tudor? Are all teachers 100 years old?
We've also got human ties. I need lessons on doing up my tie?
I hope we have lessons on spelling Beauchamps.
We might have them next term.
Oh well, I guess it's all change.

Thomas Harris (12)
Beauchamps High School

GOING TO THE COUNTRY

I had one last look back at my mum.
I was sad, frightened and worried.
Feeling shy and odd as the train whistle went,
I looked back and saw her crying.
I soon realised that she wasn't happy,
And I really wanted to cry.

Louise White (11)
Beauchamps High School

CATS V RATS

There once was a cat,
And he was very fat,
Oh very fat was he,
He ate us up,
He chewed us up, but there were three,
3 survivors meet some more,
And hatched a daring plan,
For schemers they were made to be
And never to be sad.
The 3 left were Psycho, Cagney and Leader,
Their motto was to be big and brave and bad,
That they were, there is no doubt,
They meet other rats by hanging about.
They warned them about the cat that was very fat,
They were grateful, no doubt, about that,
But the cat suddenly sprang,
And ruined their little gang.
1 more was left, the leader of the rats
Had sadly been scratched
And very slowly and painfully died against a rock
While the cats ran amok.

Nicola Lynn (11)
Beauchamps High School

STARS

S   hining, silver stars gleaming in the sky
T   winkling like fairy lights
A   ngels glittering from up above
R   eally beautiful like diamonds glistening
S   himmering silently and still.

Emma Lane (11)
Beauchamps High School

JEALOUSY

High up in the sky,
Silent in the crowd,
Until one day
You have held it too long,
That you rain down on the earth,
Letting out what's inside,
Now it's another sunny day,
You've gone white again,
Until another day,
When temptation gets too much,
It lurks in every corner,
Waiting to strike!

Victoria Bryan (14)
Beauchamps High School

WHAT IS IT?

Silently, she creeps into the night,
Camouflaging in the darkness, she sits,
waiting for her prey.
Hours pass, but still, she sits, watching
with her beady eyes.
Suddenly, she catches a female gazelle,
trotting off towards her home.
However, she is too quick to let the gazelle
go.
Now she is satisfied, she silently creeps
back home.

Tessa Krishnan (11)
Beauchamps High School

ALL CHANGE

Beauchamps? What type of school is that?
Do we give bows to champions?
And why is it a high school?
Do they stretch you until you're a certain height?

I'm entering the enormous building.
Wow, it's gigantic!
Who's that behind the glass window?
They've trapped her!
Anyhow, I walk up to the hostage,
I ask her where the office is.
She kindly said, 'This is the office.' How strange.
I ask her why she is trapped.
She exclaimed, 'I'm not trapped!'
I ask her where I should go.

In the hall I find my form.
Chairs? Don't we sit on the floor?
Everyone stands. Does that include me?
Mr Bell strolls into the hall.
He tells us to sit.
But why? I'm already sitting.
There's a screen. Are we going to watch a movie?
What, no movie?

Who's she? Mrs Shotton?
So that's what our targets mean.
She must shoot each of our targets.
Playtime bell! Oh dear!
Outside world here I come!
Why did I change schools?

Sarah Nunn (11)
Beauchamps High School

FIRST DAY AT BEAUCHAMPS

I see the school building,
I see the school doors.
I see how big the school is
With so many floors.

I step inside and feel excited,
There is the Head standing in front.
'In here for year sevens!' he calls.
I say goodbye to Mum and grunt.

I walk in the hall,
I see a chair.
'No' says the teacher,
'You're over there!'

So I sit in my group
And wait for my name.
Hey! I think.
It is starting to rain!

So at lunch
We can't go outside.
It is raining so hard
It's like a water slide!

The bell has gone,
Miss Melvin next!
She takes us for English
She is truly the best!

Well I can't say that!
She is the only teacher I know,
I will probably see more teachers,
But I now have to go!

I leave the school building
Kids talking all in a row,
Man I can't wait to tell my mum
I can't wait for tomorrow!

Ben Shewan (12)
Beauchamps High School

DECEMBER 24TH

Christmas is coming
The tree is twinkling with light
How much longer?
4, 3, 2, only one more night.

Through the window
Black, black sky
The moon, creamy custard
Stars, shining high.

What is flying in the sky?
Red, white, a sleigh?
Could it be?
Will he stop?

Please, please!
I am so excited
Tweenies, Action Man
Football kit, remote car.

Please Father Christmas
Don't be late
Please stop at my house
Number eight.

Tom Farrow (11)
Beauchamps High School

LONELINESS

Fearing the night, darkness approaches
I am alone
Rustling leaves, the cold night's breeze
I am alone
Anticipation, lurking around me
I am alone
Closing my eyes, pictures remind me
I am alone
Standing behind me, ready to enter my body
I know that I'm alone
Surprises aware me, and then they take me
Leave me on my own
Then in my mind, I hear them call me
They tell me, that I am alone.

Emma Browne (14)
Beauchamps High School

BEAUCHAMPS

B   is for best
E   is for excellent
A   is for athletics
U   is for unbelievable
C   is for champions
H   is for homework
A   is for amazing
M   is for marvellous
P   is for perfect
S   is for school.

Karen Lawrence (11)
Beauchamps High School

ALL CHANGE

Today is the day I leave my junior school
What is senior school like?
My new school is called 'Bowchamps'
Does this mean we wear bows and we are champs?
I wonder what the food's like
Will I make new friends?
Why is the school day longer?
Why do we have to wear ties and blazers?
We are doing circle time for the last time.

It's my first day at Beauchamps
All my clothes are too big
We are in the assembly hall
Why do we sit on chairs?
Everyone is taller than me, I feel like an ant
My first lesson is French with Mrs McLure
Will she tell me off?
Will I get detention?
I don't know any French, we never did it in junior school
Why don't we have one class?
French is over, phew!

About to start my lunch
I remember about the juniors
Our lunch was at 12, now it's 12.20
we have vendor machines with lots of yummy chocolate
In juniors we weren't allowed chocolate.

We now have maths, my tutor is Mr Beedham
What is a tutor?
Do they tut a lot?
School is over
I suppose it's not that bad after all!

Danielle Wilkinson (11)
Beauchamps High School

BLACK HEART, GUILTY SOUL

If you live by the sword,
You'll die by the sword;
You reap what you sow,
A tree that stands in shadows
Can never hope to grow.

If you believe in Heaven,
You'll surely go to Hell;
You've hollowed out your own grave,
You'll find it fits you well.

You've done the unforgivable,
'Sorry', will never do,
You can try to look away
- Your dark heart knows the truth,

Innocence is precious,
You've taken it away,
It's too late just to admit it;
There's a price to pay.

Stephen Howsam (15)
Beauchamps High School

CATS

Cats miaowing all through the night,
Cats sleeping all through the day,
They're weird things, cats.
Why stay awake all night
And sleep all day?
What a boring way to spend your life,
Every night and every day.

Claire Kimber (11)
Beauchamps High School

MOORS

When I look out of the window,
All I see is grey,
Horses, cows and sheep
And rolled up bales of hay.

It's dark out in the moorland,
There's nothing much to do,
If you take a glance at houses and trees,
There are very few.

It's misty and foggy and ever so cold,
You have to act strong and be very bold.
When walking around just brace yourself,

For a ghost might jump out and say Boo!
You're lucky you don't live in the moors;
I'd love to swap places with you.

Robert Williams (12)
Beauchamps High School

DOGS

A   steady highly trainable dog.
L   oving caring dog.
S   ee his magnificence as a guard dog.
A   nd see him play in the park.
T   rained to protect me from danger.
I   ntelligence from this dog is hard to believe.
A   n excellent presentation from this dog.
N   ice and playful dog.

Gary Smalley (11)
Beauchamps High School

MAYBE

Maybe I was wrong
Maybe I do need you
Maybe I do like you
Maybe I do love you

Maybe my feelings scared me
Maybe they got too deep
Maybe I wasn't ready for love
Maybe it was too big a leap

Maybe you made me happy
Maybe you made me cry too
Maybe you made me angry
Maybe I still love you

Maybe I should've listened
Maybe I should've given you a chance
Maybe I should've tried harder
Maybe this was romance

Maybe I should never have left you
Maybe it was the wrong thing to do
Maybe I was wrong
Maybe I still love you

Maybe it wasn't all my fault!

Lauren Long (12)
Beauchamps High School

BIRDS

Flapping, flying through the sky,
Feeling the cold, bitter air,
Always watching out for food,
Always knowing where to go.

Watching baby birds hatch,
Born in a hard, sheltered shell,
Nestled in a twig nest,
Nice, warm and cosy.
Just where to be!

Ruth Kadesh (11)
Beauchamps High School

DOLPHINS

Dolphins swimming the ocean wide,
flying through the sea,
I wish that I could get close to touch
all the ocean for you and me.

Crying, and calling through the air,
free to go I don't know where,
If only we could find a place,
You could see my happy face.

Nets that stop you passing by,
pull you from the precious sea,
I would never let you sigh,
So make the most of what you have.

Until the moment when you die,
The sea is kind,
The sea is true,
It will always be looking down on you.

If you had the chance to go and swim,
I wonder what it would be like,
Under the deep blue sea,
Where my mummy's eyes won't be on you.

Claire Baker (11)
Beauchamps High School

LONELINESS

All alone in a house,
With nothing much for company, just a little mouse,

The sadness,
Of loneliness.

Now you wish you hadn't run away,
For now apart you must stay,

The sadness,
Of loneliness.

The voices in your head,
You are going mad is what they have said,

The sadness,
Of loneliness.

The darkness of the room,
With just a gleam of the moon,

Depression will overcome you when you are all alone.

Hayley Barrick (12)
Beauchamps High School

TABBY CAT

A tabby cat
Her eyes are tense
In my room so dark and dense
I can't believe she sits alone
Listening to cats that roam
The dark and dense nights at home.

Samantha Pocock (11)
Beauchamps High School

SOLVE THE MYSTERY POEM

An old man found inside a bus stop,
quite dead, chalk face.

He had a picture of his granddaughter,
in a broken frame.

An old-fashioned clock in his coat,
no hands on the face.

A penknife with red ink on the blade,
with a note around it.

A notebook of names,
with two names crossed out.

A small bottle of ale,
half full.

A war medal in a box,
with a lion on it.

Blood along the pavement,
like red paint.

Peter Sneath (16)
Beauchamps High School

SUNNY DREAM

Emerging from the horizon it sparkles into the sea
Its beauty is too blinding just for you and me
And with that the world's inner beauty would have to be
The peaceful and calm sunny dream.

Kerry McCormick (11)
Beauchamps High School

ALPHABET POEM

A is for animals, some tame and some wild,
B is for ball for any young child,
C is for clowns that make us all laugh,
D is the dirt we wash off in the bath
E is for eggs you can fry or boil
F is for flowers that grow in the soil
G is for grapes, some purple, some green
H is for hives where bees can be seen
I is for ink that's found in a pot
J is for jelly that wobbles a lot
K is for kites that fly in the air
L is for lion, stroke him if you dare
M is for money you find in a purse
N is for needle and also for nurse
O is for owls, we hear them go hoot
P is for penguin in his dinner suit
Q is for queen with a crown on her head,
R is a rabbit that wants to be fed
S is the sugar we put in our tea
T is the trunk you find on a tree
U is for unicorn that cannot be found
V is for vehicle for driving around
W is the washing we hang on the line
X is the letter that's too hard to rhyme
Y is for yacht with a sail and a mast
Z is the letter that always comes last.

Emma Willis (11)
Beauchamps High School

ALPHABET POEM

A is for Amanda who lives down my street.
B is for Bernard who has smelly feet.
C is for Cara who likes to dance.
D is for Delia who lives in France.
E is for Ellie who has a swimming pool.
F is for Freddy who drive me up the wall.
G is for Georgie who likes to play.
H is for Henry who's had a good day.
I is for Ingrid who is very shy.
J is for Jessie who always tells lies.
K is for Kris who likes to talk on the phone.
L is for Layla who always moans.
M is for Mark who always gets drunk.
N is for Norris who's a seventies punk.
O is for Oliver who writes with a pen.
P is for Penelope who's got a letter to send.
Q is for Quentin who has a letter to post.
R is for Richard who likes to eat toast.
S is for Sally who has a dog.
T is for Trudy who hid behind a log.
U is for Ursula who likes to write.
V is for Victoria who got a bit of a fright.
W is for Wilma who makes a lot of noise.
X is for Xavier who plays with the boys.
Y is for Yvonne who likes to cook.
Z is for Zoe who likes reading books.

Elizabeth Brown (12)
Beauchamps High School

THE NET

I like surfing the World Wide Web,
I stay up late when I should be in bed,
Moving around from page to page,
It sometimes seems to take an age.

I sent an e-mail the other day,
A click of the mouse and it's on its way,
I hope it gets to where it's going,
But in this day and age there is no way of knowing.

The other day I downloaded a big file,
The content of which makes me smile,
I extracted the file and it's there for all to see,
My Bonzi Buddy swinging from a tree.

The Bonzi Buddy moves around the screen,
Talking to me and seeing where I've been,
It's that time of night again The Web getting slow,
It must be time for me to go.

Nicholas Flynn (13)
Beauchamps High School

MY BROTHER . . .

My brother is a bother
He's a silly little rat
He owns a silly puppet
And he wears a silly hat.

His friends they raid my room
When I am not there
But when I have a go at them
They say they do not care.

He tells tales to my mum
And gets under my feet
If I was the only child
Life would be
So sweet.

Daniel Ellis (13)
Beauchamps High School

THE FREAKY FOREST

As they crept in the forest,
All shaky and scared;
All three of them had been tricked or dared.

'What was that?' little Johnny had said.
'Don't worry about that, just think you're in bed.'

As the forest got darker,
The blood rush rose,
Until they felt a twitch on the nose.

'I'm feeling uneven,' said little girl Vic.
'I'm quite sure I'm going to be sick.'

As the trees turned to ghosts,
And the bushes to ghouls,
It felt even scarier than Niagara Falls.

'I can hear something coming, let's run away now.'
'Look, in the tree, oh no.'

'Miaow!'

Lisa Scott (11)
Beauchamps High School

DIAMONTE POEMS

Fish

Fish
Small, gold
Gulping, swimming, eating
A tail twirling reptile
Whale

Turtle

Turtle
Small, hard
Swimming, crawling, eating
A plant eating herbivore
Terrapin.

Matthew O'Neill (12)
Beauchamps High School

UNDER THE SEA

Under the deep blue sea;
Where all the creatures live;
The starfish that sleeps peacefully on the rocks;
The dolphins that swim through the sparkling waters;
The fish with their beautiful colours;
The mermaids with their long blonde hair;
The crabs with their sharp pinchers waiting to attack.

All these creatures live under the deep blue sea;
In another world unseen by you and me;
Maybe one day someone will unlock their mysteries.

Kelly Dalby (11)
Beauchamps High School

BEDTIME

Come along
It's half-past nine
Bedtime!

Homework done?
Yes Mum
Bedtime!

School bag packed?
Take your library book back
Bedtime!

Had a shower?
Took an hour
Bedtime!

Brushed your teeth
Rinse the sink
Bedtime!

Get to bed you need your sleep
Got an exam later on this week!
Bedtime!

Can I read? Can I text?
No you can't - whatever next!
Bedtime!

Good night Mum
Good night Son
Bedtime!

Lauren Pentelow (12)
Beauchamps High School

THE DRAGON ON THE HILL

There once was a great, great dragon,
That lived upon a hill.
And when the clock struck midnight,
It went out for the kill.
Its wings spread out and off it goes
Whooshing through the sky,
And when it saw its prey below
It swooped from way up high.

There was a village quite near by,
The people lived in fear.
In case the terrible monster
Ever came too near.
However, in time it came close,
And fed upon their cattle.
They need to find a brave knight
Willing to do battle.

They found a warrior, who was strong,
Enough to beat this threat.
Although he was very tough
It was his hardest battle yet.
At last he came back to the village,
With the head of the beast.
And the mayor of the area
Threw a massive feast!

Michael Garside (11)
Beauchamps High School

MY FAMILY

First there's my mum
And she's really fun
She likes to keep fit
And she's a real hit

Then there's my dad
And he's really mad
Golf is his hobby
And Mum calls him Bobby

Then there's Jane
And she's a real pain
Drives a fast car
And goes very far

Then there's Louise
And she's a big tease
Always on the phone
Whenever she's home

Then there's Matt
And he likes to wear hats
He's quite tall
And likes to play ball

Last there's Chloe
With her hair in a bow
Starting to talk
And also walk.

Lauren Buckle (12)
Beauchamps High School

SPARKLE

Horses are wonderful, horses are kind
Some don't like people, but others don't mind.

Go for a ride, get on his back
It's not too hard, once you get the knack.

Give him some sugar, watch his nose twitch
Then scratch his back, right on the itch.

Go for a gallop, then slow to a walk
Wouldn't it be great if horses could talk.

Isn't it sad when the ride has to end?
So go fetch a horse and get in the trend.

Rebecca Hadley (11)
Beauchamps High School

THROUGH THE SCHOOL GATES

Every day through the school gates,
Say 'hi' to the teachers,
Say 'hi' to my mates.
Into the class,
With tests and tests, work and work,
I hope I pass,
The snacks are lovely,
But the queues are long.
If they've got pizza, I can't go wrong.
End of the day through the school gates,
Say 'bye' to the teachers,
Say 'bye' to my mates.

Ashley Jordan (12)
Beauchamps High School

MY HAMSTER

My hamster is just like an owl
Sleep during the day
Get up during the night
She is also like a tiny rabbit munching its way through a carrot
Drinking water all the time
And making nests anywhere she can
Hamster running round the cage
Like a Kangaroo in a rage
Tries to run away from us
Like a race car in the dust
Candy is her name
Running round is here game
Soft, cute, cuddly and still
Falls asleep when she's on her wheel
And on my lap.

Christina Fenn (13)
Beauchamps High School

MAIDEN OR WIDOW?

A maiden legend sits at her peak,
Never moves, she would never speak,
Waiting for her lost love to return,
But you know she wants to yearn.
She waited there for years and years,
After she would not bear tears.
Until one day she seemed to stop,
Stuck for eternity as a statue of rock.
What do you think, maiden, widow or legend?

James Wong (11)
Beauchamps High School

SUMMER

In the summer sun
Me and my family have fun
Water fights and playing ball
Right next to the big, blue swimming pool.

The sun is so hot, round and bright
Without the sun we have no light
This makes the summer so fun and exciting
It stops me and my sister fighting.

In the summer time when the weather is fine
And all my family are drinking fine wine
Sausages and burgers cooking on the barbecue
I love summer!
Do you too?

Coral Purcell (11)
Beauchamps High School

THE WOLVES

The wolves stalk in a pack,
When they eat they rip and hack,
The prey, a wildebeest,
Will provide a tasty feast.

Birds will eat what is left,
The wolves chase them,
They consider it theft.

Nicholas Platt (11)
Beauchamps High School

CHRISTMAS

Soft snow falling slow,
Candles are burning very low.
Darkness falling very fast,
It's just like a gloomy blast.

Decorating going on,
To adults, it's the marathon.
Christmas tree going up inside,
To children, it's like a ride.

Presents being passed around,
There is a lovely, Christmas sound.
Children playing in the snow,
To them it's a blustery blow.

Carol singers are at your door,
All they want is more, more, more.
Now Christmas has gone for another year,
All the adults give a cheer!

Michael Edwards (14)
Beauchamps High School

MY LIFE

My life is like a feather on the wind.
Falling when we have a test.
Flying when we have art and drama,
Soaring with happiness and joy.

Elliot Bishop (11)
Beauchamps High School

SCHOOL LIFE

My name is Thomas I'm only eleven
I started at Beauchamps, in year seven
I enjoy the lessons, my favourite is IT
My day starts at ten to nine, it ends at half-past three
I've got my own locker it comes with a key
You can have it for a year for a very small fee.

Thomas Shimali (11)
Beauchamps High School

VOLCANOES

Volcanoes spurting lava up high,
Deadly gases rise to the sky,
Molten lava tumbles down,
Crushing every little town,
Dust is flying all around,
Until it settles on the ground,
The sky has gone as black as night,
They wonder will they ever see light?
Now the sun has reappeared,
The landscape looks all barren and black,
But soon the plants will grow back.

Ben Gotch (12)
Beauchamps High School

NEVER INVITE A FLEA TO TEA

Never invite a flea to tea,
It won't eat anything, not even a pea,
All it wants to bite is me,
So never invite a flea to tea.

Tom Thornton (13)
Beauchamps High School

Reading

R   ead quietly everybody! What book are you reading?
E   verybody listen, look at this book I'm reading, it's great!
A   ngels sounds like a good book!
D   o you want to read it some time?
I   nteresting! This chapter is so interesting.
N   o I'm not going out tonight I'm reading!
G   ather round and let me read you a story.

Alexandra Wilson (13)
Beauchamps High School

Lion

Lion,
Sneaky, mighty,
Roaring, hunting, stalking
King of the jungle
Crouching, lingering, sleeping,
Killer, thriller
King!

Jake Nutley (12)
Beauchamps High School

Tractor

T   revor the tractor,
R   aced along the road,
A   nxious enough,
C   arefully he goes,
T   urn the corner,
O   pen him wide,
R   eady for anyone to climb on and ride!

Joe Read (13)
Beauchamps High School

SORRY

Sorry about that Mum
For scribbling on your book
Sorry about that
I didn't really look.

Sorry about that Dad
For digging up your garden
I was looking for buried treasure
I do bed your pardon.

Sorry about that Teacher
About breaking the school bell
There's only one thing for it now
You'll just have to
Yell!

William Simmons (11)
Beauchamps High School

ROBOT WARS POEM

With Craig and Julia, they are the crew
Robot Wars they bring to you.
Grinding metal and sparks flying
Roboteers are really trying.
House robots try to smash and crash
You better watch out for Sergeant Bash.
Shunt, Matilda and Sir Killalot
The deadly weapons that they have got.
Pussycat and Hypnodisc they love to please
Let's get on down with Wheely Big Cheese.
Dead Metal is the robot they love to hit
If you don't then you're in the pit!

Richard Gould (12)
Beauchamps High School

THE LONELY CLOWN

As the strangers looked at the lonely clown in disdain,
They never realised the suffering and pain.
On the distraught clown's face there was no smile,
The lonely clown hasn't laughed in a while.

A clown should really be
Full of happiness and glee.
It is not right to be a sad clown
So why upon his face is there a frown?

There is more to this clown than you and I know
Why should he be full of sorrow?
What has happened to this clown to make it feel so bad?
Why is this clown looking so sad?

Megan Morris (12)
Beauchamps High School

THE LION

Walking through the jungle
Stalking its prey along the way
Pouncing on them, hungry yet brave.

Running from poachers
Feet stopping along the way
Because he sees man.

King of the jungle
Loud and proud
Yet scared.

Louise Smalley (13)
Beauchamps High School

CONFUSED

I don't know what to write
I'm really really confused
I have to write a poem
It's giving me the blues

I have to write a poem
I don't know what to say
It's giving me a headache
And spoiling my day

Everyone else is writing
They've all got good ideas
Shall I write about Dad cooking
Or Mum drinking beers?

Everyone else has finished
They're going out to play
I really don't believe it
Sir told me to stay

Playtime is over
They're coming in again
I still haven't started
I think I've lost my pen

Goodbye class
See you in the morning
Not you Hannah
You've spent all day yawning

Just get on with it child
I'm fed up with excuses
Your spelling is atrocious
And your written work is useless

The cleaners have finished
Wish I had too
I feel like crying
And I need to use the loo

The stars are out
The moon is bright
But I must be dim
Cos I don't know what to write

I've finally started
The words are beginning to flow
Is it really such a crime
To be a little slow?

Hannah Wells (11)
Beauchamps High School

LIGHTNING

Lightning is a frightening thing
You don't know what to do,
You could hide under a table
Or get blown to Timbuktu,
The rain lashes down
Beating on the ground,
The rain churning up the mud
A tall, large mound.
Drains are always overflowing
The sun never, ever glowing.

James Stretch (12)
Beauchamps High School

UNITY

(Dedicated to all who died in the American massacre on 11th September 2001)

No one knows what will happen now,
With all this awful strife.
The people who lost their loved ones,
The man who lost his wife.

The people in the towers,
Deserved not to die.
What happened to them was wicked,
All we can do is cry.

As for the people on the aircraft,
So brave they must have been.
Babies, children, adults too,
Unforgettable, but unseen.

We've been told to be prepared for war,
How on earth can we do that?
To arm ourselves with lethal weapons,
Or even a baseball bat.

I honestly don't understand,
Where all this hatred comes from.
I don't know what the answer is,
But surely it's not a bomb.

A friend of mine is out there,
What will become of him?
Someone so young and full of life,
It really is a sin!

Faye Moody (13)
Beauchamps High School

A DARK STREET

Night falls,
The street becomes darker,
Only when the street lights turn on,
The children will go in,
The street gives off an impossible threat,
Is something there, what's that I see here,
The frightened souls scream out,
An inky-black darkness,
Shows no colour about,
But if you face a home,
The darkness disappears,
The screeches and yells of cats,
Which are all chasing birds and mice,
They see right now,
Why the humans are terrified,
It's this figure outside a house,
Number two if I can see,
A big shadow,
Way too scary to be,
A monster,
A goblin,
A witch,
Only when up close they see,
Nothing to be afraid of,
After all that fuss,
It turned out to be . . . an overlarge dog,
So the children of number eight,
Creep into bed,
Go to sleep,
No more peeping at the dark street.

Dean Sambrook (12)
Beauchamps High School

MY SIMILE POEM ON FOOTBALL

Football is as exciting as the Nemesis at Alton Towers.
It is as tiring as running through the jungle.
Football is as fast as Linford Christie.
Football is as hard as doing a GCSE.
It is as loveable as Joanne Guest.
Watching Arsenal is as enjoyable as eating chocolate.
Watching Tottenham is as boring as watching paint dry.
In winter the weather for football is as miserable as
Teachers on a bad day.
In summer the heat is as hot as a burning oven.

Football is as great as the world
Football is everything!

Scott Wilkinson (12)
Beauchamps High School

THE TIGER

Slinking through the grass quietly unseen,
A predator so ferocious and mean.
When it gets to pounce,
It uses every ounce;
Of weight and power
But no ripple touches a flower,
It latches on the animal's head
And with a quick flick it's dead.
Silence falls over the plain
Where the animal was slain.

Matthew Clark (12)
Beauchamps High School

My Cold

I've got a cold,
I'm all snotty,
My nose is blocked
And I feel grotty.

Sneezing sneezing
Is all I do
Tissue after tissue
I go through.

Oh I do hope that
It won't be long,
Before this stuffy, old cold
Has finally gone.

Karen Bell (12)
Beauchamps High School

Cats

Tortoiseshell, Persian and Siamese,
All these are cats and they often have fleas.
Ginger and brown, black and white,
Moggies have the ability to jump from a height.
Kittens and moggies, kittens and cats,
Will all leave on your carpets
Half dead rats.
They can be very cute, and very, very sweet,
But it's not until you see the bill
That you know how much they eat.

Alice Catherine Beatrice Feldwick (12)
Beauchamps High School

MY GRANDAD

He was funny and sweet,
He liked to be neat,
He never seemed down,
He never made me frown,
And even if he did,
I would forgive him,
'Cause I was only a kid,
But years have past,
We have all grown so fast,
One day he just let go,
But I know,
He will always love me,
Like things used to be,
And I wish he were here,
And if he were,
I wouldn't shed a tear,
Even though it's sad,
I wouldn't cry,
'Cause he's my grandad.

Danielle Lane (13)
Beauchamps High School

FOOTBALL

F   ootball is the game we love to play,
O   ut in the sun,
O   ut in the rain,
T   ackling players left or right,
B   all flying in the sky, goal in sight,
A   ll for one and one for all,
L   aughter and tears, football has it all,
L   ove it, live it, *that's football!*

James Hibbert (11)
Beauchamps High School

MY FAMILY!

My brother is a real pain,
All he ever seems to do is play computer games.
Every afternoon he sits down on the sofa,
And just stares at the TV.
Sometimes I wonder if he's really related to me!
My dad is the best,
Yet sometimes is quite mean,
But he cooks really good food
The best you've ever seen
My mum is excellent,
She's always there for me,
However she can get very stroppy, that's when I'm not keen.
She will always give me sympathy
When I've hurt my knee.
My grandma is a first-class nan,
Plus she makes the finest cakes ever, and if you say
She doesn't, then you aren't very clever,
My grandad is really cool,
And he's the best at DIY,
Whenever I go round there
He is the first to say hi!

But one thing is for sure and it's really true
And that is I wouldn't change a thing, no matter
What you might do!
If you gave me £1,000,000 it just wouldn't be the same
As without my family around I would go insane!

Elizabeth Lucking (12)
Beauchamps High School

THE AUTUMN POEM

Tree is like a rough sandpaper bark.
Petals like dogs' ears, long and dangly.
While leaves sway to the ground gracefully.

Balkiran Atkar (12)
Braeside Senior School

LAST LESSON!

The distant sound of a whistle, whoops and yells,
A whisper in a group and eyebrows are raised,
Chairs scrape and I'm in a daze
The rustling of paper as we all gaze
Out of the window listening to the distant pitter, patter of the rain,
The bell rings, and the shuffling of feet
As we all run out into the street.

Courtney Bull (13)
Braeside Senior School

THE SCARY TREE

It is like a giant,
With monster branches,
Below are the tiny fairies.

Sachleen Chana (12)
Braeside Senior School

THE MUSICAL FIR TREE

Dainty fairies dance around the fir tree,
Dancing to the rhythm of their music,
They hold their hands and circle around the tree.

Jasmin Valera (12)
Braeside Senior School

VALENTINE'S POEM

Love is a sign of good friendship to a boy,
To love and care for them and be full of joy.
It makes you feel like you're wanted and loved,
When you're loved, and cared for from him and above.
Valentine's Day is time to be with a boy,
A romantic rose and a cuddly toy.
So I told you once,
I told you twice,
You're the only one in my life.

Lianne White (13)
Braeside Senior School

SCARECROWS

There he is, that fierce thing,
With his burning fingers of flames,
A crow comes past, and never again.

Abbie Segal (12)
Braeside Senior School

LOVE THOUGHTS

OK think? What can I say?
Would you go out with me?
Oh no, that's too pushy.
Marry me?
Oh no, that's so old fashioned.
OK, OK, he's coming over.
Here goes.
Hi . . .
This is so hard for me to say . . .
but . . . but . . .

I . . . I . . . I . . .

Think quick
Kiss me?
Oh what am I saying?

I really like you
I've seen you around
Well what I'm trying to say is . . .
Well . . .
I . . .
I love you.

Kathy Williams (14)
Braeside Senior School

THE GIANT TREE AND MINIATURE BELLS

The giant tree, his bark so rough
Looks down on the little miniature bells,
They are all pearl white with fright.

Jessica Gendler (12)
Braeside Senior School

THE ALONE TREE

That tree all alone
In the green glade
Only seen by birds.

Rosanna Hill (12)
Braeside Senior School

THE TREE MONSTER

The big monster is very tall,
The big monster has long brown arms,
The snowdrops below him are screaming like children.

Pooja Minhas (13)
Braeside Senior School

PLAYTIME'S OVER

Like a tall climbing frame, the tree towers over the fairies,
They stand, a circle of flowers with droopy heads,
Sad to go back to work.

Leena Patel (12)
Braeside Senior School

THE MONSTER TREE

Big, gaping monster
Snowdrops cowering below
Terrified . . . terrified.

Helen Reynolds (12)
Braeside Senior School

THE SUN AND MOON!

Underneath the glass eye of the moon,
Underneath the glare of the sun,
Underneath the smooth light of the moon,
Underneath the shimmering of the sun,
Underneath the sparkling of the moon,
Underneath the sweaty face of the sun,
Underneath the cold ice of the moon,
Underneath the furnace of the sun,
Underneath the condensation of the moon,
Underneath the humid shadow of the sun,
Underneath the freezing damp of the moon,
Underneath the golden fire of the sun.

Kaley Jones (14)
Brookfield House School

THE SUN AND THE MOON

Beneath the fierce fire of the sun
Below the frozen ice of the moon
Under the oppressive orange heat of the sun
Underneath the cold, white hand of the moon
Beneath the melting magma of the sun
Below the silver crystals of the moon
Under the smiling, humid, sweaty face of the sun
Underneath the sharp and jagged mountaintops of the moon
Beneath the infinite sun and the eternal moon
Burning, shining, turning forever,
World without end.

Jonathan W Stringer (14)
Brookfield House School

THE MOON

As I stand on the crackling snow of a cold winter's eve,
I watch the moon radiating its luminescent glow,
Watching its elegant gaze,
Enveloping the snow with its celestial shine,
Observing its glistening and kindly light,
Under the twinkling wink of the crystal face.
The glass sphere smiling and twinkling on the newborn snow.

David Inskip (13)
Brookfield House School

THE SUN

The sweaty face of the sun,
The burning touch of the sun,
Underneath the golden eye of the sun,
The erupting fire inside the heart of the sun,
The blinding light of the sun,
The hot breath of the sun.

Rajdip Panesar (13)
Brookfield House School

CAMPUS

C   lever smart board showing us work
A   n amazing projector
M   y one of a kind swipe card opening my locker
P   raise certificates passed all around
U   s, we are in our school uniforms
S   pecial school named Campus.

Nicky Saunders (11)
Chafford Hundred Campus

LUNCHTIME

Swipe cards in,
Open doors,
Posters flash,
Photos shine,
Friends gossip,
Enemies fight,
Lunch money out,
Organisers in,

This is all that happens after the bell,
Watch out - hungry adolescents hurdle
To catch the front of the queue.

Juliet Connell (11)
Chafford Hundred Campus

OUTSIDE

Green grass
Brown mud,

White chalk
Smelly manure,

Heavy slabs
Parked cars,

Metal bikes
Huge diggers
Working builders.

Steven Blake (11)
Chafford Hundred Campus

BUTTON

I found a button
A sparkling circular button.
It was in my auntie's bedroom
It's my cousin's
Who's twelve.

It comes from a
Glittering dress
Which comes to her knees.

She likes going to parties
Going shopping.

I'm going to keep it
And pass it down in my family.

Georgia Relf (11)
Chafford Hundred Campus

DRAGON'S COAT

Dragon's land is where I found it
It was dark big and jagged!
I put it in my pocket and found out later
It was the button of a dragon's coat
I was scared at first
But then I tried to give it back
The dragon was mean
But took the button
And said to me if I came here again
He would eat me.

Abdus Samad Azad (11)
Chafford Hundred Campus

MY BUTTON

Creamy, white and fluffy,
Was my nan's cardigan.
The button was beautiful too
Creamy, white and shiny.

She pulled one button off,
To be passed down
Through the family
To future generations.

It now belongs to me,
A blonde twenty-eight year old.
Very wealthy
Very happy
I shall pass it down.

I'll pass it down
To my daughter
When she turns sixteen
She will love it.

I shall tell her
To pass it down
So that
It goes on forever.

Amy Higgs (11)
Chafford Hundred Campus

THIS IS JUST TO SAY . . .

Dear Miss
This is just to say
I'm sorry I forgot my homework
Last Wednesday

This is my excuse
For not bringing it in
My dog messed on it
And I threw it in the bin.

James Boyce (11)
Chafford Hundred Campus

MRS LEAFORD'S BUTTON

A button was found in
A lady's house
On her dressing table.
It came off a coat
That was very long indeed.
It was flowery and colourful
Like the rainbow.

This button belonged
To Mrs Leaford.
Who was very famous indeed.
The coat was very famous indeed.
The coat was bought for her.
£250, £250.

It was bought for her son's wedding.
It shone in the sunlight.

It was a snow white colour.
It was a see-through button,
With a red flower
Stuck in the middle.
That was Mrs Leaford's button.

Charlotte English (11)
Chafford Hundred Campus

THE PRINCE'S BUTTON

How I found it
On the floor

It came from
Red velvet trousers

Its owner a boy
A king to be

A prince of fifteen
At the time

It is returned
By a man

The old king
Now has a souvenir

A gold, rounded
Old and worn button.

Tyler Betts (11)
Chafford Hundred Campus

THIS IS JUST TO SAY . . .

This is just to say
I have broken your best vase,
I didn't do it on purpose,
I was playing football in the house.

Forgive me,
I will never give Lee a table football match again.

Andrew Gilbey (11)
Chafford Hundred Campus

THE FAMOUS CHAFFORD HUNDRED CAMPUS

It's an amazing building,
cool laptops,
useful signs,
exciting books.

Some wonderful hi-tech,
flash swipe cards,
unique lockers,
jazzy smart boards.

Lots of interesting objects,
helpful timetables,
great bike racks
many diggers.

That is the famous Chafford Hundred Campus!

Natasha Rees (11)
Chafford Hundred Campus

FISH FOR MY TEA

Those fish look nice,
With mice.

Good for my tea,
Just you and me.

Good enough to eat,
A nice teatime treat.

Tasty little fish,
Sitting on my dish.

Rachel Slocombe (11)
Chafford Hundred Campus

SUNNY MORNINGS

Every morning I get out of bed
And look out the window and shake my sleepy head
The buttercups glistening in the sun's light
And will it, maybe, yes it might
The kingfisher's egg has hatched

The daffodils opening what a pretty sight
The sunflowers could reach the kites
The tulips are shining in the fresh dew
The roses are red, neat and new

The rabbits are playing in on the lands
The beavers upstream are making their new dams
The birds are singing
It's a gentle and kind ringing
It's like summer's silent whisper

But soon the flowers die off
The animals go into their homes for winter
The birds fly to the south
It's summer's silent whisper again saying 'Autumn's coming.'

Robyn Freeman (11)
Chafford Hundred Campus

BLUE

The light sparkling water
The water that flows rapidly
Thin ice in winter
A tear from my eye when I cry
Happiness.

Danielle Bolding (11)
Chafford Hundred Campus

THIS IS JUST TO SAY . . .

I am really
Sorry
For being so late.

One of my friends'
Mum
Got lost
On the way home.

She couldn't find the right road.
We got back from the netball match
At 6.30
So please forgive me
For being so late

But my friend's mum is
Brainless
So don't blame me
Blame her.

Kim Ormes (11)
Chafford Hundred Campus

MY YELLOW BUTTON

I was walking past one day,
Then on the way
I saw a yellow button,
Then I picked it up
And I put it in my cup
And walked away.

Kelsey Hawkes (11)
Chafford Hundred Campus

MY BUTTON

My button caught my eye
When one was wandering
Around a sale
The man behind the till said it was from the 1950s.

As I stared at it, it seemed to smile at me,
A large, shiny ruby
Smile
So sweet,
So silken,
I asked the man 'How much?'
'50p' he replied
I bought the button
And I went on
I thought of whom my button belonged

A famous model came into mind
So fair,
So pretty,
Look there's my button on her bag
So glossy
So red
Her bag matches my button, a red bag.

Jessica Ribbons (11)
Chafford Hundred Campus

MY NAN

Her hair is grey like a cloud
On a rainy day and as curly
As worms wriggling around
Her skin is as smooth as a shiny apple
And wrinkly like a prune

Her nails are as sharp as the tip of a spear
Her memory is as good as a stored computer chip
Her eyes are as blue as glistening water

My nan's the best!

Cassie Taiani (11)
Chafford Hundred Campus

CHAFFORD HUNDRED INSIDE AND OUTSIDE

Grass
Smooth, reflective
Short and green
Is this grass?
Yes, spring grass.

Window
Open, translucent
Shiny and clean
This is a window
Or so it seems

Digger
Dangerous, massive
Yellow and constructive
Could be destructive

Chairs
Uncomfortable and
Small,
For those
That are tall.

Fabienne Palmer (11)
Chafford Hundred Campus

CHAFFORD HUNDRED CAMPUS

The school was a building site
It was full of horrible manure
There was always builders around
It had lots of dirt
We had concrete for playgrounds

But that was when the school started
Now we've got everything we need
Good food, playgrounds and stuff
And you've got laptops and libraries
And lots of educational things

So now that our school is finished
It's better than any other secondary school.

Amanda Comer (12)
Chafford Hundred Campus

THIS LITTLE BUTTON

This little button
On my hand
Glinting in the sun
It's dazzling bright
And the colour is white
And shaped like a plum
This little button
On my hand
I found it on the street
It was from a lady sixty years old
Well that's what I was told
And that's my story complete.

Louise Brown (11)
Chafford Hundred Campus

SCHOOL

School, what is it actually for?
Do we actually learn
Or is it just to torture us?

The teachers are mad as hatters
I'm sure they're aliens.
The food is vile
It tastes like rotten cheese.

The science teacher is eerie
He keeps body parts in his closet.
The playground has walls that touch the sky
You could never escape in a million years.

The best part is leaving
The chamber of horrors.

Thomas Rogers (11)
Chafford Hundred Campus

THIS IS JUST TO SAY . . .

I have left so early, I'm very sorry.
I know we were supposed to take you out for breakfast.

But what's better, going out for breakfast
Or MTV hits! Calling you up and saying
You are going to meet O-Town and Blue today at five,
In the morning in the studio.

Forgive me I know it's your birthday
Paula is sorry too, we'll make it up to you we promise.

Kymberley Jamieson (11)
Chafford Hundred Campus

How To Cook Chips In Socks With One Match

Ingredients:
Chips
Socks
1 match

Method:
Put chips in socks
Go to kitchen
Light a match
Put socks onto match
Go and daydream about being rich
Wonder why firemen are carrying you out the front door
Watch house burn down
When firemen put out the fire go and get chips and socks
Also get plate
When outside eat socks and chips
Then realise you need tomato sauce
Go get tomato sauce
Enjoy eating socks and chips.

Craig Leddra (12)
Chafford Hundred Campus

School Poem

Strong digger
Dirty cars
Shiny bikes

Tall crane
High flats
Opaque windows
White walls

Plastic chairs
Hard tables
Black ink pens

Hi-tech smart boards
Strict teachers
Information posters.

James Allan (11)
Chafford Hundred Campus

MY LITTLE ALMIGHTY BUTTON

I found this button
On the counter,
It was in a bookshop
Where I'd never been before.

It's olive coloured,
An almighty size.
It's very obsolete,
I'm sure it's from a cloak.

'What will I do with it now?'
You ask.
'Why, take it back to where I found it,'
I answer.

I'm hoping that no one comes back for it,
Then it will always be
The little almighty button
That I found on the counter in the bookshop.

Laura Brealey (11)
Chafford Hundred Campus

THE BUTTON

Old woman about eighty years old dropped a button
Pretty girl found button
Pretty girl looked at button
Button is gold, circular, patterned
Pretty girl put button in loft
Button never out again!

Ross Carmichael (11)
Chafford Hundred Campus

THE BUTTON

I found my button in a charity shop,
It's turquoise and white and lovely and bright.
I think it belongs to a lonely old lady,
50-60 her age.
I think it's part of a gleaming, thick cardi,
That the dear old lady loved.
What shall I do with the delightful button?
I know, I'll give it to the shop keeper.

Jenny Keeble (11)
Chafford Hundred Campus

HOMEWORK!

I haven't brought my homework in
'Cause my sister threw it in the bin.
I know it's bad,
So please don't be mad.
I'll make sure I put it in my bag,
And I'll bring it in tomorrow, Miss!

Celen Hurbas (12)
Chafford Hundred Campus

MUD CAKE

Ingredients needed

About five cups of mud
500g of sugar
500g of flour
500g of butter
500 of egg
Half a cup of milk
Vanilla essence
Give a good mix you can use a blender.

Method

Sieve the flour
Whisk egg
Whisk sugar and butter until turns white like ice cream
Add whisked egg to sugar and butter
Add sieved flour bit by bit until wraps up the egg
Add vanilla essence to give a nice smell
Children fight in the kitchen and knock over mixture, tell them off
Because ran out of mixture, go to shop and get double mixture
Just in case it happens again
Go home
Make mixture again
Put in oven for thirty minutes, at heat medium
Watch television for an hour
Smell burning!
Open kitchen door if got one
Put burnt cake in bin
Use spare mixture
Make again
This time watch TV for twenty-five minutes
Take cake out after five minutes
Eat and enjoy.

Gerald Carew (11)
Chafford Hundred Campus

BY THE LOCKERS

I am by the lockers,
What do I see?
Sharp, green metal lockers
And a dark green furry floor.
I can hear lots of children,
Talking, eating, laughing and reading.
Here comes the teachers!
Hide all the food, put it in your lockers!
Oh dear they are now all shouting,
We all have to go out in the cold wind.
All the children run to the dining room.
Nice and warm.

Letty Ho (11)
Chafford Hundred Campus

MY BUTTON

My big, round, golden shiny button
was found in an office on the floor.

My patterned button came off
A posh lady's jacket, long sleeved
Aged between thirty and forty years of age.

I am going to keep
This gleaming button
To remind me
Of my day trip to London.

Michaela Joynes (12)
Chafford Hundred Campus

The King Of The American Jungle

Everyone knows the king of the jungle
He has a button with a star in the middle
It looked like a face of a lion
And without this button he would only be half lion

Once I was walking through the jungle
And I found the glistening button
I thought hard what to do with it
Sell it and make money, or hand it back to the lion

I think I would give it to the lion
But I thought how much money I would make with it
It is so important to the lion
So I decided to give it back.

Amar Mistry (11)
Chafford Hundred Campus

The Magic Button

Horizontal gold stars, black background with silver brim,
That was the button I found in the wood.

It must have belonged to a wizard with a blue cloak.
He must have lived in the wood.
It must have been from when he was teleporting
To buy ingredients for a potion.

I put it on my own cloak and walked off home.

Adam Yates (11)
Chafford Hundred Campus

THIS IS JUST TO SAY

This is just to say,
I didn't come to practice because . . .

My brother broke his ankle,
And was rushed to hospital,
To have it checked out.

My aunt came over
And made us eat horse hay
Saying it was good for us. (Yuck)

I was in a robbed store,
And was taken to
The police station for questioning.

I twisted my ankle,
Aliens abducted me,
I was a part of a secret mission.

Oh what's the use
I didn't come to practice
Because I was grounded
For making excuses to a teacher
And I'm sorry. So . . .
Can I please play in the match?

Natalie Mohile (11)
Chafford Hundred Campus

THE CAR

I have done something very bad,
I need a beating off my dad.
I nicked the car,
I've not gone far.

Sorry, Dad
I've been quite bad.
I'll make it up when I get back,
I'll even put my coat on the rack.

Kane Kenyon (11)
Chafford Hundred Campus

ESCAPE TO HIDE OUT

You're mine fish face you're mine
I'm hungry dear don't mind
You'll never escape,
Never on this planet's face.

I need to think of a plan
Oh good, look at that fan
If I overflow my tank
I will escape,
'Cause a certain seat is blank
And there I will hide.

I'll get that fish
No doubt, because you can't
Run about no doubt.
If it somehow escapes
I'll never let it race.

I'm now out of my tank
I'll escape now from this place
If I can hold my breath
To the brink of death
I'll make to hide out.

Tapiwa Sanyauke (11)
Chafford Hundred Campus

THE SCHOOL

The fields are long,
The houses are tall,
The tables are wide,
The chairs are small.

The books are large,
The folders are blue,
The teachers are annoyed,
And the dictionaries are good for you.

The smartboard is smart,
The laptops are exciting,
But because they're so smart
People start fighting.

And now I have
Finished my poem
I would like
To sing goodbye.

Steven Mitchell (11)
Chafford Hundred Campus

THIS IS JUST TO SAY

This is just to say,
Sorry I am late,
I did not wake up until
Half-past eight.

So please forgive me
For being so late,
I really had forgotten the date.

Sophie Lynott (11)
Chafford Hundred Campus

FOGGY WHITE

White, misty and kind of small,
Coiled, coloured and ice cool.
Glistening, shiny and very bright,
Reflects the moon in the night.
Fell on the floor and went for a stroll,
With mud on, it looked quite dull.
I picked it up and went for a walk,
Then its shine started to stalk.
I took it home and added it to my pile,
I looked at it once more then I started to smile.
It shined white as bright as a light,
Filled my room so it was bright.

Joseph Yeomans (12)
Chafford Hundred Campus

MY SPECIAL BUTTON

Whilst looking through my washing
I saw a shining stone,
It glittered in the light,
How beautiful it looked.
I had seen this stone before,
it was the Queen's crystal gem.
The Queen had bought it in a very posh store
But when she finds out it's gone
I'll be in trouble.
What will she say?
What will I do?
But I don't want to be the one
Who she's telling off.

Hollie Samantha Kerr (11)
Chafford Hundred Campus

THE LOST BUTTON

Circular, glistening, cloudy blue
At the bottom of the streets
At an old restaurant

I bent down to pick it up
And it shone right into my eye

So I took it home
Went upstairs
And looked at it closely

To see how shiny
It was and went to find its owner
I found an address in the ashtray
So I went to find out

I knocked on the door
And no one was there

Then I saw a car
Parking into the drive
She looked at me
In a cheerful face

And then I thought
Maybe she didn't want it
So I gave it to my nan.

Still thinking why wouldn't
She want a glistening button
Like that?

Leanne Brooks (11)
Chafford Hundred Campus

THIS BUTTON

This button,
I found in my garden.

This button,
Is very old.

This button,
Is golden and curved.

This button,
Is gleaming and patterned.

This button,
Has a creamy bit in the middle.

This button,
Is it a bank lady button?

This button!
What am I going to do with it?

This button!
Is going to the museum.

This button!
I'm going to ask who would have worn it!

This button,
Is for a lady.

This button is
Special to *me!*

Mia King (11)
Chafford Hundred Campus

SCHOOL

Before I came to Chafford Hundred Campus
I was really, really excited,
But when the 6th September finally came
I was really nervous about coming to a hi-tech school!

I'm still worried now
Because I don't want to go to the
Wrong lesson by mistake.

I am very proud to be a pupil at
Chafford Hundred Campus
Because it is such a hi-tech school
With our swipe cards.

Ashley Watson (11)
Chafford Hundred Campus

THIS IS JUST TO SAY

This is just to say,

I'm sorry for playing so bad,
I've really broken my leg (not)

I'm not good at football
I went blind (slightly)

Forgive me Manager
You are the best (as if)

I'm not blind anymore
And I fixed my leg.

Regan Comer (11)
Chafford Hundred Campus

CHAFFORD HUNDRED SCHOOL

The school is the best,
better than all the rest.

You won't be bored at any time
because there's always something to do.

It's where the teachers work hard
and are always on guard.

The cleaners keep things clean,
wherever we have been.

Chafford School rules!

James McGrath (11)
Chafford Hundred Campus

IS THERE ANYTHING WORSE THAN THIS?

I was working at the sewing machine
I looked out of the window and saw a scene
Oh dear, this is my worst fear.
My stitching has gone crooked,
My teacher looks wicked.
Here I am now
With my teacher who looks foul.
In detention
'Pay attention!'
What a horrible day.
Well that's all I can say!

Laura Whitbread (12)
Great Baddow High School

WORLD WAR III?

Five planes hijacked
How could this be?
Many a person
Tried to get free.

Two of them dumped
In the World Trade Centre.
One of them crashed
Near Pennsylvania.

For one, the Pentagon
Was its aim.
One that disappeared;
There wasn't a game.

And so I leave you
With the story,
In which none other
Could be more gory.

Gemma Cope (12)
Great Baddow High School

MY FRIEND

Whenever I turn around and smile
She's always there to give one back
And as a friend she's never lacked
The one thing that makes me happy
Is that she's always there
If I am ever in trouble
She turns all my problems into rubble
And that's why she's my friend.

Allison Wisbey (13)
Great Baddow High School

PEOPLE

Why do people stand and stare?
Why look and glare?

Why do people not care?
Why are people so unfair?

Who is to blame?
And what's their name?

This is not a funny game,
But there must be someone to blame.

Whose fault is all this?
Please give me a list.

What is the evidence to show?
Whilst the fact are low.

Which man in this how
And how do you know?

What will happen next?

Hannah Underwood (12)
Great Baddow High School

THE ROSE BLEW

There in the distance, the roses blew
Waiting to be picked in the light of the moon.
Their red blooming petals had attracted the eye
Of a young boy who lived nearby.

Abigail Watson (11)
Great Baddow High School

THE STARS

The stars are brilliant and beautiful,
The stars are bright,
The stars are like white dots in the black night sky.
The stars form shapes which make up the zodiac,
The stars are comforting,
The stars are wonderful,
Everybody likes them.
They light up the night sky with their friend the moon,
When the sun comes out you can't see them anymore,
But they are still out there in the universe.
The zodiac is brilliant,
If you are born in February or March you are a fish,
But if you are born in December you are half man, half beast!
And if you are born in another month you are something different.
I think the stars are cool,
And there are many out there in the big universe.

Robert Smith (12)
Great Baddow High School

MATT, MY BEST MATE

When I turn around he's always there,
With his smile and his glare.
No matter where he'll be,
Always standing just by me.
Never one to turn his back,
A helping hand he never lacks.
Helping me when I'm down,
Worth more to me than a million pound.
If he would leave,
I'd be lost . . .

Ashley Reeman (13)
Great Baddow High School

TRUE LOVE

I met him through a friend of mine,
I didn't know him well,
I'd given him the eye and introduced myself,
And that moment in love I fell.

He lived near me,
Coincidence or what?
And so I met him up the park,
I was with some friends of mine,
And we flirted until along came dark.

Before I went home he gave me his number,
And I gave him mine as well,
We said goodbye and left the park,
I felt like I needed someone to tell.

That night we started to get to know each other,
By the use of text,
We told each other the way we felt,
So I asked what would happen next.

He replied, 'Will you go out with me?'
And I answered his question with 'Yes!'
Even though he was two years older,
We'd be good for each other nevertheless.

We spent so much time together,
And we became so close as friends,
But more importantly, close as a couple,
And this life I wish would never come to an end.

Sam James (14)
Great Baddow High School

I'VE ALWAYS WONDERED!

I've always wondered what it's like
When you come to the very end?
Death puzzles me, it's odd!
Why do some people go in pain
And others go peacefully?
I've always thought you see the light
At the end of the long tunnel.
Hopefully you'll go to a better place,
That's what my mum always says.
Some people die old and others young
You never know when your time's up
So make the most of your life.
Sometimes you know, like when you have an illness
You are just waiting, waiting
Hoping it will be a quick end
Hoping you'll be spared of pain.
Others don't know -
Are taken suddenly
In a bombing, are shot, or run over.
I hope I'm taken in my sleep
I just go to sleep and never wake up
I imagine my spirit leaving my body
Floating away like a dove.
I don't believe in suicide
It's like giving up your soul
You don't want it
As if it's not precious.
I used to be scared of death, not anymore.
My poem probably sounds weird
But I've always wondered - haven't you?

Jenna Grigg (14)
Great Baddow High School

LIARS

Doesn't it annoy you,
When they think that they're your friend.
When they turn around, hit you hard so you can't breathe,
And lie right to the end?

'I swear on my life'
'I swear on my life'
Is what she always said,
Then you decide to believe them,
But their lying out of their head.

Another friend says,
'Gem, it's true, please believe me.'
You think, which one do I believe?
Who would never deceive me?

You're in your room,
Trying to think it through,
Who shall I believe?
What shall I do?

It's happened before,
With a close friend of mine,
Is she jealous of me having other friends,
Or does she lie all the time?

My best mate, a liar.
Well, is meant to be.
Why does she have to do this,
Every single time to me?

I'm never going to believe her,
Ever, ever again.
This is the way women feel
About the lying species - men.

Gemma Aston (14)
Great Baddow High School

TERRORIST ATTACKS ON NEW YORK CITY

Only fools with no hearts
could kill those people
Cowards who would not own up

Many people died from those planes
in the sky
New York shrouded in smoke
and confusion

A time of great sorrow for the brave
and the loved one's lost
But also a time for the world to unite

The terrorists, however hard
they may try
Will not crush American pride.

We all will bounce back stronger
and more determined
To strive together to bring
a world solution
In dealing with these dangerous people.

Emma Martin (11)
Great Baddow High School

FAST AND SLOW

Slow is like a turtle
trudging around in a jungle.
Slow is like a toddler,
toddling around on hands and feet.
Slow is an old woman walking along,
slow, slow, slow,
very slow.

Fast is like a person
racing on their bike.
Fast is like a car on the motorway
speeding 100 miles an hour.
Fast is a plane landing at Heathrow,
fast, fast, fast,
extremely fast.

Andrew Martin (12)
Great Baddow High School

THE GIRL

The girl is the one who I am fanatical
about.
The girl is the one who I sit and stare at
when I'm feeling
sad.
The girl is the one who I feel is
faultless.
The girl is the one who I turn to
when I am troubled.
The girl is the one who I like to
solemnize my joy
with.
The girl is the one who I unknowingly
and constantly upset.
The girl is the one who I crave to
be with.
The girl I am in love with is
called
Emily.

Terry Hambling (12)
Great Baddow High School

SUNSET

Down it goes over the horizon, far, far away
The red glow of the setting sun
Soon would be gone
Until it rises once more again.
What a beautiful sight to see from a distance
The colours, the brightness
Will take your heart away.
Approaching nightfall
As the evening flies by
It gets lower and lower in the sky
Knowing that evening will soon turn to night.
The sky gets darker and darker
No more that friendly glow
Only the tip of the sun remains above the horizon
Then you have one last glance at it
Before it's gone!
Gone! Gone!
The light has finally fallen
And night is with us once more
For the sun we will not see until another day!

Alex Brown (12)
Great Baddow High School

THE LADY FROM BEIJING

There was a lady from Beijing
who really loved to sing.
She got in her car
and went quite far
'til her phone went ring, ring, *ring!*

Hannah Herlihy (11)
Great Baddow High School

AMERICA

People working in the Twin Towers
Everything is silence
Nothing going wrong
It is now 9 o'clock
Then, coming from nowhere
Four American planes come
Then one hits the left tower
And another hits the right tower
They are on fire
Another plane hits the Pentagon
Another is shot down into the fields nearby
The President is taken to New York
The fire brigade is there
People high up jumping out of windows
People also trapped and can't move
Everyone screaming
New York filled with smoke
People crying
Relatives in the building
People being burned
Tourists stuck and can't go home
It was a real nightmare.

Graham Jones (12)
Great Baddow High School

CATS

C   ute, cuddly, curious
A   dorable, active, agile
T   errific, tremendous, turbulent
S   oft, surprising and purrrrfect!

Fiona Carter (12)
Great Baddow High School

THE SETTLE TO CARLISLE RAILWAY

It's one of the three wonders of Northern England,
From the town of Settle, north of Leeds,
To Carlisle on the Scottish border.
The railway goes uphill as it climbs,
Reaching a hill with the first of 14 tunnels,
It then goes over Ribbleshead Viaduct,
The longest on the line.
It then goes through
Blea Moor, the most deserted place on the line.
Blea Moor tunnel is the longest on the line.
The line goes through two Yorkshire Dales, Garsdale and Wensleydale.
It goes over some more viaducts until it gets to Dent,
The highest mainline station in England, 1050ft above sea level.
The line descends a bit,
Then it climbs up to Aiss Gill summit, which is 1069ft above sea level.
When the train gets to Appleby it stops for a photo stop, while another
                                                              train passes.
When the other train has gone,
The train goes over a series of tunnels and viaducts
All within one mile of each other.
The line's steep descent goes into a more gentle slope
Along the Eden River with its gorge,
Which was the hardest part to build.
The railway joins the west coast mainline
Just before the station at Carlisle where the line finishes.

Stephen Horne (12)
Great Baddow High School

MY PHOBIA

I have a fear of soap and water
I hate to wash but Mum says 'I ought-ter'
I reluctantly wash behind my neck and ears
I'm told soap hasn't been there for years and years.

Now that I am nice and clean
I feel like causing a right scene
By splashing around in muddy puddles
And causing Mummy lots of troubles.

Richard Button (11)
Great Baddow High School

GOD BLESS AMERICA

Tall, beautiful, outstanding as the sunset
Master of the skyline
That you see from the seas.
Suddenly, so suddenly,
A Boeing 607 plane struck the first tower
People were accidentally pushed out of windows,
As others gasped for breath.
People cried, whilst others died.
Rescue people arrived,
But at the same time, another Boeing claimed lives.
The second plane, (a Boeing 737) was steered at over
200 mph into the second tower.
More tragically were killed. Men shouted.
Women cried. People were jumping.
At long last, the one thing that people had dreaded
For many years had come true.
The first tower collapsed into a pile of concrete and rubble.
Then, shortly after, the second tower collapsed.
People dashed for cover.
Bush declared war.
But the main thing is that many died,
The Twin Towers are no longer there.
But terrorists are still here, in every country.
There is no escape.

Simon Want (11)
Great Baddow High School

FEAR

There are many different types of fear in the world
Like phobias, ghosts and many more.
Do you know that fear is where you try but you can't scream?
All that comes out is a silly squeak
That's the fear you get when you see a ghost.

The phobia fear is when you cannot run
But you stand there screaming, staring at the
Spider, dark, height or a rat!

All the other fears include,
Scary stories, graveyards at night, vampires, witches
and haunted houses.
But real fear comes to you
when
someone's
in
your
room
and
shouts
Boo!

Jamie Lawrence (12)
Great Baddow High School

GHOST

G   oing through the creepy hallways
H   ouse to house he goes
O   pening doors and going through walls
S   caring everyone on its way
T   error house is where he scares!

Natalie Turner (11)
Great Baddow High School

Terrorism

Terrorism is a very bad thing
As on telly you have seen.
I think the culprits should all be killed.
Loads of people have been
Very, very upset by this attack.
I don't know anyone out there
But for those people who do
They wonder how the culprits dare.
To attack something once is one thing
But do it twice, that's another.
Some people lost their dad
Some people lost their brother
Some people lost their mum
Some people lost their sister.
For the people who survived
They came out with burns and blisters.
This is a catastrophic event
It's worse than some twisters.

Matt Roberts (12)
Great Baddow High School

Animals

A   nimals all over the place
N   oisy little things
I   nteresting with a funny face
M   aking lots of holes in the ground
A   ll the slimy, slivering bugs
L   ike to slime and sliver about
S   o many annoying weird-like sounds.

Sammi James (11)
Great Baddow High School

ME AND MY LIFE

I am tall but not cruel,
People say I act like a fool,
I don't care at all.
On weekdays I am taught,
In my spare time I play sport,
Tennis, football, golf or pool,
I like to play them all.
Me and my best friend Liam,
People say they never see 'em
Without the other one!
They say we're inseparable,
Even when we're in a swimming pool,
We both go and enjoy Scouts,
But not so much when Eagle shouts,
That's a poem all about me!

Jonathan Hammond (12)
Great Baddow High School

MY POEM

H aunted houses everywhere
A t night-time all things scare
L oud whispers in the air
L ow voices here and there
O gres scurry round the ground
W illows sway, but make no sound
E very ghost in this fair land
E njoys the . . .
N ight that the witches planned.

Rebecca Scofield (11)
Great Baddow High School

ENGLAND'S 5-1 WIN

They said we can't do it,
But we're gonna prove them wrong!
Cos we are top of the table
Now that Keegan's gone.
Michael Owen, can we score it?
Michael Owen, yes we can!
Sven and the gang have no doubts
Working together, we can beat the Krauts.

Only six minutes in
And we were one nil down.
The Germans thought that they had won,
Our faces all wore a frown.
When Owen scored his first,
We all started to smile
Cos we were going to beat the Germans
By a mile.

Michael Owen, can we score it?
Michael Owen, yes we can!
Sven and the gang had lots of goals
But none of them were by Paul Scholes.
Gerard scored
Owen got two more.
We had knocked the Germans
Down to the floor.
The smiling Swede
Started to grin
Cos then he realised
We were going to win!

Matthew Steele (11)
Great Baddow High School

BROTHERS AND SISTERS

B rothers are brats
R ough and tough
O dd everywhere they go
T roublemakers
H it their sisters
E at all the time
R ude and disgusting
S piteful and gross.

A nd sisters are:
N ice and cute
D arlings every day.

S trong sisters
I ntelligent and smart
S weet and kind
T reasures everywhere
E veryone likes us
R eally nice to Mum and Dad
S o that is the way we are.

Pembe Hill (12)
Great Baddow High School

THE LAST MOMENTS IN THE USA

In the United States at 9.03am
Some people were filming for the TV
When all of a sudden
The building fell down to the count of
1 . . . 2 . . . 3

What caused this to happen? I wonder how?
We saw a plane come crashing down.
It was mayhem in the building
As people were panicking.

People were jumping or would die in flames,
And everyone would run, thinking that this is *no* game!
The man who is behind this, wanted to destroy America
We think he already has!

James Bishop (11)
Great Baddow High School

My Dog

I have a dog called Jenny
She's 14 years old
She's not worth a penny
But to me she's worth gold

When she comes in a room
She sometimes even makes a fume
It makes a disgusting smell
I think I may have gone to hell

I have a dog called Jenny
She's 14 years old
She's not worth a penny
But to me she's worth gold

In the morning she wags her tail
By the door she waits for the mail
Sometimes she can be a real good laugh
But runs whenever you mention 'bath'

I have a dog called Jenny
She's 14 years old
She's not worth a penny
But to me she's worth gold.

Jason Howard (12)
Great Baddow High School

SAILING AWAY

Sailing on the deep blue sea,
Sailing with a nice cup of tea,
On the deep blue sea.

Sailing into the sunset,
Sailing with a bet,
On the deep blue sea.

Sailing in a gale force wind,
Most made out of tin,
On the deep blue sea.

Sailing stared,
Sail flared,
On the deep blue sea.

Mast snaps in pieces,
Put on the thermal fleeces,
Over waves we sail,
Down waves we fail,
Wind goes into vales,
All calm
On the deep blue sea.

James Tovey (12)
Great Baddow High School

A WALK BY THE RIVER

R   ushing waterfalls shimmer
I   n the light of a morning's sun
V   iolets sway in the breeze
E   merald leaves
R   ustle as if laughing and having fun.

Anna Crampton (11)
Great Baddow High School

THE CLOUDS

The clouds are very special to me,
They're fluffy and white,
And sometimes a miserable grey,
They float around Earth,
Without a care in the world,
You can see them from above,
And see them on the ground,
In winter it's cold,
They come down to the ground,
And suck them back up,
They're always around,
These fluffy white clouds,
My friends, my pals,
Those fluffy white clouds.

Simon Beard (12)
Great Baddow High School

THE BLACK ROSE

The petals of the black rose
are as dark as a cold winter's night,
and as soft as the wind's gentle breeze
blowing against your face.
Its stem is a beautiful colour
with thorns like dragons' teeth
to protect it in the wild.
Its strong roots are like anchors
digging into the seabed,
that hold the roots firmly in the earth.
The wonderful plant glistens in the sun . . .
    the black rose.

Jay Poulton (12)
Great Baddow High School

CHRISTMAS

Christmas is a happy day,
Christmas is a joyful day,
All the presents we open,
All the roasts that get eaten,
Hear people singing,
My phone starts ringing,
Have a merry Christmas,
I know she'll miss us,
My auntie's gone to America,
I hope she'll have a merry time,
I got a new computer,
It's got a good feature,
The design was wicked,
This was the best Christmas,
And now it's all over.

Lee Kirby (12)
Great Baddow High School

RHYS

Small, black, curly hair, Rhys my dog
I wonder where?
Always there, prepared for anything.
Early morning, late at night
you were there without a fright.
Little Rhys, I still miss you, your spiky collar,
your black hair, always aware what is there.
Even though he put you down, you are still with me
I want you back but I know it's impossible
for you were murdered from such innocence
of sharp, white teeth.

Edward Williams (11)
Great Baddow High School

CONFUSION

Him and me
love?
Her and him
love?
Her and me
hate!
Me and him
love?
Him and her
love?
Me and her
hate?
Confused!

Joanna Goddard (13)
Great Baddow High School

MY SISTER IS A BLISTER

My sister is a blister, not sweet but sour
and she thinks she has lots of power.
The power that exists was a sweet, little bliss
but never fear every time my big brother's near
his blessed little powers seem to appear.
They rumble and they humble
had me in a jumble.
But when pulled apart by Mum
they were sucking their thumbs.
I am the good one says my mum
and if I don't do what Mum wants to do
What's done is done
go suck on your thumb.

Christina Elane Loveridge (11)
Great Baddow High School

THE ROCK 'ARD CROC

Twisting
Turning
Attacking
Evil
Cunning
Sharp
Tough
Scaly
Quick
Sly
Hunter
Dark
Clever
The rock 'ard croc is after you!

Sam Hawker (11)
Great Baddow High School

FRISKY

He sat around in his cage all day
Until I came home from school to play
Yes we had fun and played all day
But I think he's gone to a better place
I have a photo of him next to my bed
I have a think about where he's gone.
Far away in a distant land or high in
The mountains or in the sky.
Flying on clouds he watches me
Oh I miss my hamster Frisky!

Katie Bluck (11)
Great Baddow High School

MY FAMILY

My dad . . .
>Really hair
>Sometimes scary.

My mum . . .
>Curly hair
>Groans like a bear
>But a mum who really does care.

My sister . . .
>Will eat anything to put in her tummy
>But she's very funny.

My brothers . . .
>They are a real pain
>But they're exactly the same!

James Hill (11)
Great Baddow High School

THE MATCH

He took it past them all
as he ran with the ball.
They fell to the floor
with their mouths as wide as a door.
He got to the edge of the box
where they tried to pounce on him
like a fox.
He took the shot
which went past the lot.
It hit the pole
and went in the back of the goal.

Daniel Kelleher (11)
Great Baddow High School

CATS

Cats, cats, they like to scratch
Cats, cats, they like their rats.
Cats, cats they jump up and down like an acrobat
Cats, cats, they also like to claw the mat.

Some are tame
Some are wild,
No two cats are the same.
Some have short coats, some have long.
If they eat enough food they'll become big and strong.
Their eyes help them to see in the dark,
Their ears pick up at the sound of a bark.
They are playful, funny and serious too
They love to play games with me and you.
If I was a cat I would like a good home
So I wouldn't be left all on my own.

Adam Lyons (11)
Great Baddow High School

THE BIKE

My name is Mike
I have a bike,
I ride it every day to school.
Then one day I had a fall
I grazed my knee,
When I hit the tree.
So up I got
And went home for tea.

Michael Forman (11)
Great Baddow High School

PERFECTION IS . . .

Perfection is the memories of my dog
Perfection is the star-birth representing
My friends who have died.
Perfection is the path to Heaven
Perfection is the twinkling stars we look up to,
Perfection is the life of my memories.

Perfection is the gently waves lapping on the shore
Perfection is the dolphin who swims out to save me,
Perfection is the fun of making sand castles
Perfection is the great fun I have swimming in the sea.

Perfection is the unspoiled sunset,
Perfection is the new baby I hold.
Perfection is the magnificent colours of the rainbow
Perfection is the baby animals that have just been born.
Perfection is the blossom on the trees and the newly growing flowers.
Perfection is nature.

Perfection is the world God made.

Frances Wightman (11)
Great Baddow High School

HOW TO BE A BEST FRIEND

You have to be kind
You have to be funny,
Compassionate and true,
You must not lie and be horrible.
That is how my best friend is.

Leah McKoy (11)
Great Baddow High School

A CAT HAS NINE LIVES

A cat has nine lives
It loses one when juggling knives,
The cat now has eight lives
It loses one when it tries to dive.
The cat now has seven lives
It loses one when it naughtily drives.
The cat now has six lives
It loses one when it tries to fight two tribes.
The cat now has five lives
It loses one when it tries to get four wives.
The cat now has four lives
It loses one when it tries to get to rising fives.
The cat now has three lives
It loses one when it attacks beehives.
The cat now has two lives
It loses one when it doesn't like school and skives.
The cat has one life
It loses it when a bad disease is rife.
Now the cat has lost all his lives.

Declan Crace (11)
Great Baddow High School

SPORT AT SCHOOL

We do lots of sport at school
Even though I am very tall
I don't like maths or witty verse
I can think of nothing worse

In the summer holidays
I don't get time to sit and laze
I am thinking of the games we've won
And all the time having fun

Now back to school for basketball
The game I hate most of all
So give me any other sport
And I'll work hard for my report.

Mark Thompson (11)
Great Baddow High School

WAR IS HELL

War is hell all right, I should have thought of that
before I signed up for the army.

As I made my way through the jungle with the rest
of the platoon I felt sick and dizzy and strengthless.
It was my nerves.
I felt so nervous that I could just drop to the filthy
ground and die.
I started to think about why we start wars and kill
people because our country doesn't like their country.
At that minute, I suddenly heard shouting and bangs
and saw blood flying into people's faces.
The Sergeant was shouting to everyone 'Get down!'
At that second I dropped to the floor and started firing.
It was hell, I heard screams getting louder and people
crying, people shouting.
I saw people getting shot in the head, people running
behind trees, people jumping into bushes.
I then saw my best friend get shot right under my very nose.
I was so shocked and upset, I screamed for help, but nobody came.
I heard no talking, no noise at all,
I was alone.
No help. Just alone.

Jason Schott (12)
Great Baddow High School

TEACHERS

Some teachers are cool
Some are mean
Some are nice
Some give you homework!
Some give detentions
Some are tall
Some are short
Some are girls
Some are boys
Some are strict
Some are funny
Some make lessons fun
Some make lessons boring!
Some are French
Some are Spanish
Some are German
Some are English
Some are smart
Some are not!
Some teach maths
Some teach science.

Rebecca Brunning (12)
Great Baddow High School

OSCAR MY PUPPY

O scar is my Labrador puppy
S oft is his fur
C ute is his face
A lways, he is at your feet but . . .
R unning is what he does best!

Natalie Dench (12)
Great Baddow High School

MANCHESTER UNITED THE BEST

Man United are the best
They're better than all the rest.
They score so many goals,
They break the goals.
Their manager's the best,
He leads them to glory.
All those cups and trophies
They won't have any room left.
They never foul
Unlike those nasty old Gunners.
Man United are so good,
They could beat all the other teams put together.
They are so rich, they look so good.
They make millionaires look poor.
That's my poem about Man United,
You're now probably all excited.

Ryan Fuller (12)
Great Baddow High School

HEDGEHOG

Spikes as sharp as butcher's knives
Covered in a crispy, crunchy brown-leafed colour.
Trudging through the dewy grass
To find a safe hostel to spend the day.
Also search for a tasty prey
Through the deep darkness goes
The hedgehog with his woes.
Finally he finds a leafy shelter to sleep
And as darkness thins, his sleep begins.

Natasha Tranter (11)
Great Baddow High School

MY FISH

My fish left me last week
It went to another place.
I began to cry
My first ever pet it was.

But why did it have to happen to my fish?
My parents asked if I wanted another.
I said no.
How about a different pet?
Still no.
It was my fault
I should have fed it, cleaned it out more often or something.
But I knew it was my fault.
Still I know it will be in a better place.
No other fish can replace Gerri
I will never forgive myself
Never!

Becky Hobbs (11)
Great Baddow High School

DREAMS

Dreams are where people do not suffer
Dreams are where people live in harmony,
Dreams are where drought is no more
Dreams are where starvation is no word.

Dreams are where people can drink water that is clean
Dreams are where people don't have to carry a gun,
Dreams are where people sleep with a roof over their heads
Dreams are where people do not have to fear.

Dreams are where black and white, old and young live in peace
Dreams are where people eat, drink, live and sleep together peacefully
Dreams can happen,
Dreams can only be made by us.

Jack Pridmore (11)
Great Baddow High School

PE

I hate Monday mornings,
I wake up with a sickly feeling
in my tummy.
My mum calls up the stairs
'Breakfast is ready!'

So I get up
Get dressed
Pack my bag and run downstairs
to see mum.

Mum says 'What do you have first?'
'PE,' I struggle to say
as I eat my toast.

I hate PE, don't ask me why,
I just do.
As mum pulls up at the gate,
I jump out of the car.

She says
'Have a nice day?'
I look up to see Coach Wigam
standing there.
Fat chance I think!

Louise Tredget (12)
Great Baddow High School

DOLPHINS

Under the deep blue sea
In the middle of the ocean
We come up to jump and flip
Making loads of splashes

Backs arched up then diving down
Our backs glistening in the sun
The sun reflecting on the waves
The sea horses rippling over our backs

It's nice seeing people who like us
As their little boat bobs up and down
We like to see how close we can get to them
And saying hello by creating a splash

Silly fishermen trying to hurt us
Or trying to capture us in nets
Trying to track us down with radars
Cruel weapons that shoot us

It's a horrible life, trying not to get shot all the time
Knowing you're not safe sleeping
Knowing you're not safe swimming
Knowing you're not safe playing.

Stephanie Belbin (11)
Great Baddow High School

HALLOWE'EN DISCO

They're down in the wild wood
deep in the trees,
dancing and prancing
341 elbows and knees,
as scary music floats up on the breeze.

There's a trio of zombies
howling a tune,
as a grisly ghost is starting to croon
in the bright, chilly light of the
Hallowe'en moon.

Emma Hyland (11)
Great Baddow High School

AMERICAN CRISIS

Now the Twin Towers are gone
And the terrorists have won.
America is declaring war
To get back at them, and more.
Whilst some families are mourning,
Others are taking note of the warnings.
From England we send good wishes and cheer,
Whilst you in America are full of fear.
In England we're trying to support,
And you'll always be in our thoughts.
The aeroplanes were flown into the towers,
And the pavements are laid with flowers.
All over the world it was on the news,
No matter which channel we choose.
Whilst I lay in my bed, comfy and warm,
People are working right through to the dawn.
To find what people may be left
To find the bodies of the dead.
I hope and I pray
That maybe some day
Some good will come from this evil.

Sarah Curtis (12)
Great Baddow High School

THE BEGGAR

As he rubs his feet
Gathering dirty looks, hair full of soot
A scarf and a robe are his only clothes
As he seats himself on the stony floor
He gains a penny and begs for more
He carries his life in two small shopping bags
Everything he owns is in tats or rags
He opens his bag to reveal an apple core
And finds a peanut on the floor
He walks as he chews, scuffing his shoes
He gazes into a shop window
Out comes the owner and away he is shooed
He sloped down an alley, tightening his scarf
He crawled into a soggy box, tearing it in half
He shelters from the rain hold paper
above his head
Wishing he was not alive but indeed, dead
As youngsters pass they laughed at him
He hung his head in shame
He hoped somebody his luck would change and
not every day would be the same
He fell asleep dreaming, hoping not to wake
Hoping the Earth would swallow him whole
Every part of him ached

Be grateful for what you have and hold
your head up high
Or someday you might regret the things
that passed you by.

Holly Aston (12)
Great Baddow High School

THE LOST TOWERS

Cheerful faces, laughter
Happiness in the air.
A beautiful skyline against the morning sun
Gasps of wonder at the glorious construction.
One hundred and seven floors it was
A very long journey in a lift,
An achievement to get to the top.

Suddenly it happened,
A jumbo jet collided with the first tower.
Screams and smoke filled the air,
Desperate people jumped from windows
Onlookers, frozen in terror.

Another detonation - the second tower struck,
The ground shook violently, like an earthquake.
It tumbled down like a pack of cards,
Then silence . . . silence.

There, through the smoke
Terrified, injured people emerged.
Families lost, parents and children dead,
Lives changed forever.

The World Trade Centre ruined,
Just rubble covering bodies.
The Manhattan skyline changed forever.

Nicola Standley (12)
Great Baddow High School

ANIMALS

There are many animals
Living in the world,
Orange ones with stripes and pink ones with curls.
Everyone is different
None of them the same,
I want to see them all again, again, again.
From tigers to rats
From giant whales to cats,
They live all over the world
Animals everywhere.
Asian elephants
Highland cows
Laughing monkeys
Russian hamsters.
To me they would all make
A wonderful pet.
So this is why I want to
Become a vet.

Kellie Deacon (11)
Great Baddow High School

TWIN TOWER TRAGEDY

The jewel of USA
Stand proud as the sun rises,
Hurrying colleagues flow from street to street
Calmly and peacefully going about their day.

Contracts made, then abruptly ceased,
Suddenly panic and fear rears its head.
Final thoughts, frantic calls,
Love, unknown disbelief.

Faces everywhere, on car windscreens
Railings and in memories.
To some this was a way to win a game,
But no for this pack of cards.

Peace in the end?

Samantha Prince (11)
Great Baddow High School

THE TWIN TOWERS OF AMERICA

The history will go down
Of a city, not a town.
That America lost two towers,
But the world lost more than that
When they fell, they left a pile
Which symbolised the power of hate.
All around there's lots of feelings,
Such as sadness, hope and hatred.
But we have to understand why they did it
Because they did it for a reason.
Over the years
They were rebuilt
But were made for two reasons
To put life normal again.
The first was of hope
To resist the temptation of retaliation
And the second was peace.
So it never happened again
And then we will learn to think before we act
About how it will affect others.

Alex Bulman (11)
Great Baddow High School

MY HOLIDAY

The journey was very long
And also very boring,
Suddenly I heard my favourite song
And realised it was morning.

There were swings, slides and climbing frames,
Party dances now and then
Making new friends with unusual names,
Who had to be back by ten.

There were visits here and visits there,
Big walks around the lakes,
Lazing on the beach without a care
With crisps and Coke and cakes.

Sadly it is time to go now
But we will be back again.
We have all agreed and made a vow
It was the *best!* Despite the rain.

Sandra Morrell (11)
Great Baddow High School

MY BROTHER

My brother is cheeky,
My brother is smelly,
My brother is small,
And doesn't have a big belly,

My brother is stupid,
My brother is Jack,
My brother annoys me,
And runs like a little brat,

My brother is blond, just like the sun,
My brother is sometimes so much fun,
My brother is lazy, just like my dad,
My brother is crazy, just like a lad!

Becky Elizabeth Pardoe (13)
Great Baddow High School

A SMILE!

A smile is infectious, it passes like a bug
Smiles say so much, just like a hug.
I was walking down a road
And I was passed a smile
In one second this smile could pass a mile!

This is a sign of friendship
Sort of like a code.
All the way along the street the smile really flowed
On and on, it never stops
In your house, even in shops.

I smiled again to carry on the chain
I wonder who started this, who is to blame,
A smile passes everyone
No one is left out
It's up to you if you decide to go out
To pass this smile on to someone else.

So go on, you know you want to
Go and smile and someone will smile at you!

If you feel a smile start, think of how it evolved
Let's start a chain and get the world involved.

Clare Little (13)
Great Baddow High School

THE ACCOUNTANT

Two times two is four, three times two is six
That's what she thinks as she eats her Weetabix.
Money, cash, clients, dosh,
That's all she thinks about as she has a wash.
Miles per hour she converts to how far
She can travel in her big red car.
When she arrives, as early as poss'
She gets a warm welcome from her friendly boss.
She goes straight to her work of such difficult sums,
Whilst her clients sit in their offices, twiddling their thumbs.
Plus, minus, take away and divide,
The townsfolk are all mystified
And would give up and despair;
All except for the accountant, with the short brown hair.
Her eyes are hazel and shiny and bright,
Even though she is up almost all the night.
Counting the planets and galaxies and stars,
And calculating the distance from Earth to Mars.
The accountant is skinny and pale
And is certainly the opposite to a whale.
Whenever she goes out with her friends
She spends and spends and spends.
She usually buys books and a pen
So that she can add it all up again.
She is the accountant, and everyone loves her.

Yvonne Lyman (12)
Great Baddow High School

Rain

The sky was blue and bright
I saw the shadows of the leaves dancing
There was a distant mist out far
There was a pitter-patter and a rumble of thunder.

The rain was coming
I could see it, hear it.
The sky turned black and cold,
The shadows of leaves had gone
Instead they were dripping.
The mist disappeared instead
There were black clouds.
Instead of laughter, just the slow
Patter of rain.

Jenny Field (11)
Great Baddow High School

Tortoises

Tortoises are slow and steady
When foods around they're always ready
They all have shells that are bright green
With sleeping, they are very keen.
When they are scared they hide away
Preparing for another day.
It's fair to say in every way
That tortoises are great!

Lucy Dean (12)
Great Baddow High School

STARTING A NEW SCHOOL

The night before I couldn't sleep
I was the first one up, so I had to creep.

In my new uniform I looked smart,
I couldn't eat breakfast, not even a tart.

My brothers and sister wished me luck,
They filled my bag with lots of tuck.
Photos taken
I was really shaken.

I meet my friends, we stand and chat
Then in our forms, we are all sat.

My first day had started
From my new friends
I didn't want to be parted.

I have to go, I'm too busy you see
For the rest of the year, I'm going to be
A year seven!

Laura Hunt (11)
Great Baddow High School

THE MATCH

Football's great, it's my favourite thing
I can't wait to get on the pitch
I'm in position on the centre line
And my feet begin to twitch.

I pass the ball out to the wing
And run off down the line.
I shout out to my team mate
'Come on, that ball is mine!'

We're charging forward towards their goal,
Their defence is rather poor.
We walk around their right back-man,
And take the chance to score!

We end up scoring three more goals,
Our team work's really showing
And in five more minutes of this game
The whistle will be blowing.

Dane Revell (11)
Great Baddow High School

STARTING A NEW SCHOOL

When you start a new school
the homework for you
gets bigger and bigger and bigger.

When you've started the school
and you've been in their pool
the swimming gets harder and harder and harder.

When you've had a detention
next time pay attention
and try not to get one again, again or again.

When you're lost in school
do not worry or cry
tell a teacher and your worries will be over.

When you've finished at school
and you've learned all the rules
you'll be bigger and wiser and better.

Tim Read (11)
Great Baddow High School

THE AMERICAN TERRORIST ATTACK

The sadness, the sorrow
The pain and horror
As the terrorists struck
The world is not the same.

No one knows why
We all wanted to cry,
As the two World Trade buildings fell
The world is not the same.

A lot of people died
A lot of people cried.
Everyone was in disbelief,
The world is not the same.

People jumped,
People cried,
People shouted,
They also died.
The world will never be the same.

Eve Partridge (12)
Great Baddow High School

THE LADY FROM YORK

There was an old lady from York
Who was very partial to pork
When she started to eat
She began with her meat
And it all fell off her fork.

Vicky Juniper (11)
Great Baddow High School

THE EAGLE

The eagle is strong, mighty and high
Looking down from the place where it flies.
Swooping down as quick as a flash
Hoping to catch . . .

Its beady eyes are daring and quick,
Staring down hard, heavy as bricks.
Its giant wings shine in the sun,
Looking down on everyone.

As it slows down to land
The eagle turns round
And see his prey
Which is waiting, today.

Sarah Parnell (12)
Great Baddow High School

TERRORISM

Terrorism is a terrible thing
They know what feelings these incidents bring.
They won't stop until their job is done,
They won't stop until their battle is won.
They risk their lives and others too
But they will do what they feel they have to do.
People get hurt from the dust and the dirt,
That fall from buildings so very tall.
Some people recover, but that doesn't excuse
The terrible behaviour these people can use.

Davina Mixture (12)
Great Baddow High School

VALENTINE

I have to admire you from afar
Cos your mum drops you off
   in her snazzy red car,
You've got lovely hair with a
   cute, little curl,
But my friends say you run
   like a girl,
They say you're a fake and look
   like plastic,
But as for me, I think you're
   fantastic,
You're bottom of the class, but
I don't care, with my help you'll
   soon get there.
We could meet in Zeus, perhaps
   on a Wednesday.
I don't really care what my
   friends say!
I'll be on the dance floor all alone
   with a pink carnation and a
   mobile phone.
I've named the place, you set the time
   Oh, will you be my Valentine?

Laura Southgate (12)
Great Baddow High School

AMERICAN TERROR

11th of September 2001
As the picture unfolded, the whole world was stunned.
Suicidal hijackers took over the planes
To accomplish their mission for political gains.
Chaos, terror and fear were the feelings on board
As the aircraft struck through the towers like a demonic sword.

Fires and explosions as the world stood in shock
As the towers crumbled into a pile of rock.
Lives have been lost and families ripped apart
The tragedy went straight to our heart.
The American people are rising from the debris
It is the land of the brave and home of the free.

Ashkon Meshkati (11)
Great Baddow High School

SANTA

Christmastime has come
It's that time of year
Christmastime has come
Santa Claus is near
People tell some Christmas jokes
Make some jolly snowmen
Through the stores the buyer pokes
Here's a present labelled 'To Ben'
'Ho, ho, ho!' shouts Santa
'Look at Rudolph's nose!
Go, go, go! shouts Santa.
Look how fast he goes
See that lovely tree
What a strong glow
Oh look what they've left for me
Come on boys, its time to go.
That's a whole days work
Well it is for Santa
Never watch him lurch
You wouldn't want to tamper
That's the work of Santa.

Antony Reardon (12)
Great Baddow High School

CHICKEN THIEF

Eyes like steel
afraid of the light
when he sees it
he runs through the night
with his prey, his favourite meal
chicken!
She used to scuffle round
the yard eating what she finds.
But what she didn't want to find
has finally found her and it wants
chicken!
The farmer gets his gun.
Run farmer run!
Bang! Bang! Bang!
Die chicken thief!

Lee Brobson (11)
Great Baddow High School

AMERICA TERROR

People set off just like any normal day
Not knowing what tragedy therein lay
Suddenly a huge aircraft hits the Twin Towers
Thousands of innocent people dead and trapped
Amongst huge amounts of rubble.

Hundreds of grieving relatives lives changed forever
Not knowing what they've done to deserve this
These horrible, nasty people deserve to suffer
Just like many are now.

Katie Timmons (11)
Great Baddow High School

THE SNOW HORSE

There was once a horse
Who galloped round a course.
Swiftly and stealthily
His jockey was extremely wealthy.
He ran like the breeze
With the greatest of ease.
He was a lightish grey
The snow horse they would say.
He won the race
At a terrific pace,
As he was given his rosette
Someone cheered as they'd won their bet.
Then he was proudly led
Into his cosy straw bed.

Rachel Overington (12)
Great Baddow High School

FRIENDSHIP

Friends will never leave you
Friends will never go
They will always understand
And let their feelings show.

Yes, friends will have arguments
Yes they'll scream and shout,
But you'll always find, when you
Need them most,
Your friends will be about.

Louise Curley (12)
Great Baddow High School

MY RABBIT

He was black and white
And had floppy ears.
We did everything together
Apart from one day I flooded with tears.

I found him on the damp grass
Lying as still as a log.
I poked him several times
But he didn't even jog
It had happened he was dead
Something I was always going to dread.

So there it was, Harry was dead
I shall never forget my old best friend.

Matthew Standen (11)
Great Baddow High School

WORLD WAR II

Planes come blazing
Nothing is grazing,
On the fields down below
The planes start to bellow.

Flames turn yellow
As planes come shooting down
Germans frown,
As their numbers go down.
The Germans are bombed
The fighting has stopped
As the last of the German Army is dead.

Darren Kemp (11)
Great Baddow High School

EXPECTATIONS

He's behind me, breathing down my neck,
He expects so much from me,
I have nothing,
I try and try to impress him,
But everything I do,
I'm still a failure,
Never living up to his expectations,
What does he want in a girl?
Not me obviously.
Should I change myself?
No.
He should accept me for me,
If that's not good enough,
Tough.
Move on.

Natalie Jones (13)
Great Baddow High School

ELLIE

Ellis, Ellie, she is so fine,
that is because she is all mine,
she runs around,
rolls on the ground,
she chases her tail like it is a toy,
and eats all the mail.
She plays with her toy mouse
and traipses it round the house.
She is my cat . . .
She sleeps on the mat!

Victoria Cook (13)
Great Baddow High School

TERRORISM IN AMERICA

The famous Twin Towers are now no more
Some planes were hijacked
They fell down to the floor.
As the world watched in horror,
The first tower was hit
Not expecting the second,
The world had a fit.
The third hit the Pentagon
The fourth crashed in Pittsburgh.
How much longer will the terrorism go on?
All those innocent people who went to work
Are now trapped under a pile of dirt.
I feel so sorry
I feel so bad,
I am now feeling very sad.
Thinking of what those people did
Makes me feel really sick.
All the firemen and policemen did their best,
But now we must let those people rest.

Stephanie Hayto (12)
Great Baddow High School

BROTHERS

Why did God make brothers?
They are so annoying,
They shout at you and beat you up.
They make your life a misery,
They break the vase and blame it on you
And I think to myself
Why did God make brothers?

Lucy Baker (12)
Great Baddow High School

MY FRIENDS

Sometimes I feel like people just don't understand me.
To be quite frank, I prefer my friends.
I could never be without them
And I don't think they are aware of how much they mean to me.
When I am with them, they make me feel special
And brighten up my day.
Like a warm welcoming fire that never goes out.
They make me laugh when they know I'm sad,
And smile when I'm crying.
They are like a warmth around me that never goes away
And if it did, what would be the point of life?
Who would be there to comfort and support,
To hug me as good friends so often do?
But I can always rely and depend on them
And they are always there, no matter what.
If they left me, it would be like a hole through my heart,
Which could only be mended if their warmth returned.
I'd just like to say that I love you all,
And that you are all so, so special to me.
                                        Thank you.

Francesca West (13)
Great Baddow High School

THE HAUNTED HOUSE

There is a house on top of the hill
No one goes in because it makes them squeal
One day someone went through the big double doors
Someone else watched from a safe distance
But that person heard some *roars!*
So he ran with no resistance.

Liam Collins (11)
Great Baddow High School

MY SORT OF SCHOOL

School is a place I visit a lot,
I go there to learn, well, that's the plot.
Some people bike, or go there by car,
Few people travel from lands afar,
At break they play football, run around and play,
'I wish I could be out there,' I hopefully say.
I convince myself I'll be out there in a few weeks
I turn and go as my wheelchair squeaks!
They are lucky to be able to run.
Living my life's not much fun!
As I am disabled, with a squeaky chair,
Sometimes I think life is not fair.
I cry out loud for needed help,
Ignored, sad and lonely I felt.
But I hold my head high
Proud and tall
As some day I know I will have a chance.

Greg Kuhl (12)
Great Baddow High School

ONE TUESDAY MORNING

When I woke up one Tuesday morning
Sun shining through the glass
A beautiful day, there was no warning
Of what would come to pass.

With my friends we watched in horror
As the nightmare then began.
The towers burning, screams of terror,
We watched them as they ran.

Like dominoes falling in a row
I watched the towers drop.
The streets were full of dust and dirt
It almost made me choke.

When I woke up that Tuesday morning
Life seemed free from cares
But now the days are full of sadness
America - in tears!

Katy Morum (12)
Great Baddow High School

HOMEWORK

Homework
Dreaded homework
Everybody hates homework
I've got English homework
Maths homework.
Homework
Everybody hates homework
Science homework
Art homework
All this dreaded homework
No computers
No football
None of this till homework's done.
Homework
Dreaded homework
Everybody hates homework.

Robert Barrett (12)
Great Baddow High School

CARS

There are so many cars to choose from
I'd be lost in the choices for years.
There's Ferraris and Porsches
By golly, they're gorgeous.
There's Vauxhalls and MGs
They're speedy like MCs.
It's all good talking about sports cars
But with a six member family
We wouldn't get far.
I've realised, everything's so much clearer,
What I need is a Galaxy or Zafira.
Something with many chairs and lots of boot space
And people passing by, could see the proud look on my face.
It's all good talking about nice big cars
But with my wages
I'd be lucky to get a Fiesta.
Ahh! I have the perfect one
It's not a Toyota or a Citroen . . .
It's a Volvo!

Now what about car insurance?

Chris Winch (13)
Great Baddow High School

NOBODY CARES

Nobody cares what I think
Nobody cares if they hurt me by calling me names;
Nobody cares if I'm all alone with no friends
Nobody really wants to be my friend
Altogether nobody cares.

Charlotte Clark (11)
Great Baddow High School

THE SUPPLY TEACHER

This is the lesson that everyone's been waiting for
Not having our maths teacher because she's ill,
We had everything planned.
First we would act innocent, by being really nice,
Then we would start doing what we wanted.
We would start eating gum and other sweets,
Then we would jump around on each other's seats.
Afterwards we would throw paper at the teacher,
To put her in the gloom,
Until she runs away.
Then we would cram everything into a tray
To make the room spotless
So that when the headmaster comes in
He would think that the teacher was having a mental breakdown
So we would be innocent.
But there was only one problem, when we sat down in maths
Our normal teacher came in
She said 'Good morning class, how are you doing?'
And then everyone moaned,
Our day was ruined.

Luke Venn (12)
Great Baddow High School

FRIENDS

Friends are always there for each other
No matter what the situation is,
They don't laugh or make fun
When that friend is in pain and suffering
Having friends is really great
When they play games together or make them.

Lauren Smith (11)
Great Baddow High School

I'D LIKE TO TELL YOU . . .

I'd like to tell you
a story about me.
It might sound quite boring
it's exciting you'll see.
For it starts in the garden
I was having lots of fun
when all of a sudden
some aliens came!
They strung me and dragged me
into their aircraft,
and up stepped their leader
he looked at me and laughed.
'I don't see what's funny,'
I said in a huff,
and kicked him with surprising strength
and spoke, 'I've had enough!'
I opened the door.
I broke into a trot.
I turned round and gasped in horror
for the aliens were there, the lot.
I sprinted hard and sweat poured out
and dripped down as I frowned.
But then I tripped, I think it was stones
and fell on to the ground.
Along came the guards, guns pointed at me
and parted into two.
For down the gangway was their leader
with his gun dripping with goo.
He pointed it at me and pulled the trigger
and out came a lot of grass!
I noticed I've been daydreaming
and broke into a laugh.

Matt Esser (12)
Great Baddow High School

THE SIMPSONS

Then there's Homer . . .

Homer, Homer Simpson,
He's the greatest guy in history.
From the town of Springfield,
He's about to hit a chestnut tree.

Then Marge . . .

Marge, Marge Simpson,
She has massive blue hair.
With her purple Dyson,
Oops! She hoovered up a teddy bear.

Then comes Bart . . .

Bart, Bart Simpson,
He's the naughtiest boy in the class,
Wears the same clothes,
He fires his catapult very fast.

Now Lisa . . .

Lisa, Lisa Simpson,
She's the brains of the family.
She loves reading.
But she failed in PE.

And last, there's Maggie . . .
Maggie, Maggie Simpson,
She sucks her dummy.
She's always falling over,
And then she loves to hug her mummy.

All these make up the Simpson family!

Samantha Hill & Sophie Ainscough (13)
Great Baddow High School

THIS WORLD

The pain and suffering
The neglected lives
Why does the world have to be like this?
The death, the disease,
The starvation and pleas,
Why does the world have to be like this?
Insanity, torment
Delusions and torture
Why does the world have to be like this?
The murder and agony
The rape and controversy.
Why does the world have to be like this?
Putrid, self-centred,
And inconsiderate.
Why do people act like this?
Cruel and harsh
Abusive and vain,
Why do people act like this?
Immature, phlegmatic
And crestfallen
Why do people act like this?
I would tell you the answer to my questions
If only I knew what it was!
One thing I can tell you
And this is no lie.
The dreams of this world
Will slowly fade and die.
All we can do is stand and watch!

Francesca Wells (14)
Great Baddow High School

PIZZA! PIZZA!

Pizza! Pizza!
You're wonderful food
I love you pizza
I can't eat enough
You're covered with cheese
And sprinkled with ham
Pizza! Pizza!

Pizza! Pizza!
Flat as a pancake
Round as a wheel
What choice is there today?
Pepperoni, anchovy, pineapple.
Pizza! Pizza!
Oh let me choose.

Pizza! Pizza!
Let us ring an order
Two medium sized
Two different toppings
Delivered by bike
Pizza! Pizza!
Hurry up, please!

Pizza! Pizza!
I love you a lot
You're tasty and tomatoey
I gobble you down
Oh, I can't eat enough
Pizza! Pizza!
You're wonderful food.

Luke McGuigan (11)
Great Baddow High School

ANIMAL RIGHTS

Nature is a wonderful thing
With others it may make them cringe
Because they are the stupid obstinate type,
And think they are vicious and bound to bite.
However, I can tell you it's not that bad
If you think about it, it's quite sad.
They are frightened of you.
If not then you are probably in a zoo.
Think, a stranger to the dominion
You could be so harsh, but I would be solemn.
So try and become an animal lover,
And please don't say 'Why bother!'
Animals could do with an easier life,
And what's the point of having a strife.
This is a note to all like me
Keep going and don't hurt a flea.

Richard Horton (12)
Great Baddow High School

WEST HAM FAN

Today I watched West Ham
I do so when I can
Today they were victorious
They were absolutely glorious

You can never call it boring
Watching Di Canio scoring,
I really got excited
As they beat Newcastle United

Hutcheson scored our first
I leapt up, fit to burst,
He scored with a diving header
Which I thought was very clever.

Kanoutè scored our final one
Then I knew the game was won
Soon they will play again
I will see them then.

Craig Williams (11)
Great Baddow High School

SANDWICHES

Sandwiches bore me,
They're dull
They're glum
They're not fun.
Sandwiches bore me.
You can talk of crust
Which tastes like rust.
You can talk of pork
Tastes like cork
Sandwiches bore me.
Some fillings are nice
Like sugar and spice.
But who wants that?
Not even a rat!
I hate sandwiches.

Matthew Coates (12)
Great Baddow High School

LOVE

What is it?
Where does it come from?
The heart? The soul?
Does it start with hatred
Or is it instant?
How do you know it's there?
Will you ever find it?
It could be lost?
Make it found.

Helen Towers (14)
Great Baddow High School

NO HOME

She has no money and nowhere to live,
And food to her baby she cannot give.
She'd spare her life for her son,
Living on the streets is no fun.
She tries to survive fit and well,
Where she comes from nobody can tell.
She sleeps in the alleys and no one will care,
She has no shoes, her feet are bare.
She shelters from the thunder and rain,
All over her body, all she feels is pain.
She cries for help and begs on the street,
Until a girl comes along and then they meet.
She asks for some food to feed her son,
And the little girl hands her an ice cream bun.
She thanks the girl who goes on her way,
For there she feeds with nowhere to stay.

Amy Cole (11)
Hassenbrook School

SPACE

Space
The final frontier
A place without sound
A lonely desert
Where stars are born
An empty place
Crowded with galaxies

Space
Where no man has ever gone before
Where all things move
At a million miles an hour
Where time is forgotten
A ruler is needed
For yet no king has been crowned

Space
The destiny of man
The biggest adventure
Still not conquered
A never-ending trap
Where no other life forms
Have been known to live

Space
Earth's last salvation
Space shall never die
But our planet shall
Earth, the country of death
Space, the town of life
And our last hope.

Thomas Robinson (12)
Hassenbrook School

A WOMAN'S WORK

A woman's work is never done,
And it's not exactly great!
A woman's work is never fun,
And is something that most women hate!

Always ironing the clothes,
Always doing the washing.
While the men get fun with the hose,
You never catch them near the cleaning!

Whenever they are out of the house,
It's because they're doing shopping!
Always cleaning out the pet mouse,
And the kitchen floor needs mopping!

Having to rush the kids to school,
But they're always never ready,
While dads can always act the fool,
It's up to Mum to keep things steady!

A woman's work is never done,
And it's not exactly great!
A woman's work is never fun,
It's something that most women hate!

It's something that *all* women hate!

Hannah Southgate (12)
Hassenbrook School

I...

I work with your imagination,
Your deepest thoughts too.
I smell boredom a mile off,
I sense it before you.

I trigger your daydreams,
So you can leave this world.
I let you go to any place,
Be any boy, any girl.

I am your passport to Heaven,
Your escape route from Hell.
I know your deepest secrets,
And I know them well.

I can mentally trap you,
Inside your head.
I am a friend with your conscience,
Who I know you dread.

I may only be damp air
Floating around in your skull,
But I can be any colour possible,
However, bright, however dull.

I am a thin mist
That you will never see, never find,
I am a part of your life,
I am:
Your mind!

Chloe Flame (12)
Hassenbrook School

PHYSCO

I'm scared,
I'm on the street,
There's a physco following me.
Where is he?
I don't know,
I just want to go home.

Now I'm lost,
No way out,
Do I scream?
Do I shout?
I look behind,
I think he's gone
But I'm wrong,
He's coming at me.

No way out,
Do I scream?
Do I shout?
Too late, he's got me!

Stephen Rowan (12)
Hassenbrook School

MASK

The way I stare may scare you,
I don't know if I will hurt you.
Am I dangerous? - Maybe.
Do I fill you with fear
Or is it a reflection of yourself you see?

In my distorted face,
You can see my mind.
My confusion and conflict are on display.
Yours are hidden by whatever mask
You are wearing today.

The internal fight goes on
Inside your head, unseen.
The drama is etched on my features
My mask has been
Snatched away.

Ben Sullivan (12)
Hassenbrook School

THE WALL

I was only year 7,
but it still happened.
It was always there,
blocking me,
blocking me from a
good life.
People always put it
there,
bringing it closer and
closer.
The names they used
to say,
the way they used
to laugh.
It came closer and
closer.
The nights were easy,
I could cry all by myself -
No one knew,
no one cared.
Why was it done?
What did I do?
Why me?

Laura Knight (12)
Hassenbrook School

THE STORM

The angry waves smashed up against the shore
And crashed at it ferociously
More and more.

An empty beach, no one to be seen,
Seaweed washed up on the shore,
Slimy and green.

A small boat out at sea bobbed up and down,
People on board screamed,
They feared they might drown.

The seagulls flew far away,
They wouldn't return
For another few days.

The sky was dark, it was almost black,
A rumble of thunder,
A lightning flash.

Rain started to fall heavily
From grey clouds that covered the sky
For as far as you could see.

It turned bitterly cold, noisier than a train,
Too much water
To fit down the drain.

Then fog came in, all grey and brown,
Even if you're a cheery person
It would've been enough to make you frown.

But then, all of a sudden it stopped,
Just like that,
The boat out at sea no longer rocked.

Hannah Shilling (12)
Hassenbrook School

THE LAUGHING SKULL

At last free
Free from the prison
The torture of my life
For once I might be happy

The people who caused this are standing around my resting place
But why had they never cared before?
Can't they just let me be
Or do they want me to be miserable?
Like they did before torturing me in my grave.

But instead they cry, the tears of guilt running down their faces
They should be happy for me
Do you think I would do this to myself if I had no reason?
Yesterday you were more worried about your job

If they did notice me why not tell me?
Treat me like a human being
But instead you made my life a living hell
But it's too late now, so instead I will laugh,
                            laugh in the face of death
But I also laugh at you

Now you know how I felt
Guilty, because I felt I had done something to upset you
But know if you think you have committed murder
At last something to laugh about
So *know* I have learnt to laugh at last.

Gary Shilling (12)
Hassenbrook School

FRUIT MAN

Here I sit made of fruit.
But I think I am rather cute,
Hair of grapes - red and sweet.
Banana barges are my feet.

My mango fingers taste divine.
My arms were once the finest wine.
Cox's apples are my ears.
My knees the juiciest William pears.

My beating heart, a tangerine.
Each elbow a small clementine.
As I pass you'll smell fruit punch,
But please don't eat me for your lunch.

When people walk I feel afraid.
Don't want to end up lemonade.
I hide myself in the bowl between,
a satsuma and a nectarine.
I've survived this time - I mumble.
Next time I could be apple crumble.

It's not so easy being fruity like me,
Being so delicious - so tasty.
So if you see me - let me be.
You don't really need your Vitamin 'C'!

Danny Nicklen (13)
Hassenbrook School

LAUGHING SKULL

Laughing at their pain
It's driving them insane
With those big empty eyes
It can hear all their cries

Looking at the skull
The blackness fills the hole
Looking at the jaw
Seems like an open door

So many cracks
It resembles train tracks
Without its nose
It really, really shows

Looking at the skull
The blackness fills the hole
Looking at the jaw
Seems like an open door

The skull looks so white
It really is a fright
With teeth so long
The mouth looks all wrong

Looking at the skull
The blackness fills the hole
Looking at the jaw
Seems like an open door

Matt Sandy (12)
Hassenbrook School

THE END OF THE ROAD

There's no way out,
I have nothing left,
This is the end,
The end of the road.

Heavy rain pounding on the car,
Dry taste in my mouth,
Reach for the bottle,
Ahh, sweet alcohol!

Feeling dizzy,
Tears in my eyes,
I have nothing left,
I have reached the end.

Must keep eyes on road,
Don't crash . . . not yet,
Life's not fair,
Life's not fair.

Wife has left me . . .
So many lights,
Keep eyes on road,
She doesn't love me.

Wipe tears from my eyes,
Memories flashing through my head,
Eyes getting heavy,
Drifting away . . .

This is the land where I want to be,
I have reached heaven,
Nothing can go wrong, nothing,
I am safe from reality.

This is a dream, it must be,
But I am in heaven,
The world of alcohol,
No, must wake up, back to reality.

Open eyes, over the cliff,
Falling, falling,
This is the end, I tell myself,
The end of the road.

Joe Wilson (13)
Hassenbrook School

THE SHADOW OF DOUBT

In a doubtful world of sadness
I wake to see nothing,
Just everlasting dark.

There's someone there I don't know who,
He's watching, but I see nothing,
Just everlasting dark.

Where am I? What am I doing?
Who's here? I see nothing,
Just everlasting dark.

He knows who I am, and what I do,
But I can see nothing,
Just everlasting dark.

'Help' I scream but no one hears,
What shall I do? I see nothing,
Just everlasting dark.

Geneviève Beard (12)
Hassenbrook School

THE STORM-GLOAZER

Through the misty depths of jungle
A queer storm began to tumble
Over the mountains of snowy fountains
It flew its way across the sunlit desert
The Storm-Gloazer was approaching
And that was a bad omen

In the valley withered with vines
It covered dusk with plenty of time
Up, up into the air
Passing the rivers
Passing the oceans

The merchant called Huggle
Leapt from the stern
Crossing the deck in the nick of time
What he saw were clouds of bubbles
Moving towards him on the double

Huggle was a sky-sailor on his ship
Wind Jackal was the name and it's wasn't very big
It hovered in the sky just Huggle's little rig
It stumbled a little before the abyss

The storm assembled into one big block
It flew up and down
It seemed as though the ground was going to rock
In the middle sat a black pit
A wind whistled by the ship
Rocking it to and fro.

Huggle struggled to get up
As the ship held on by the skin of its teeth
He grabbed onto the helm and turned 'til it broke
He turned to the stern and threw down the anchor
They span madly until the chain went taut.

The ship was struggling,
But the anchors were holding
Huggle pulled out his knife
And threw it swift

The wind died down
A scream could be heard
Then . . .silence
Now all that could be heard was the rustle of a light breeze
And the thudding of the ship's propeller.

Shaun McIntosh (13)
Hassenbrook School

THE RAINBOW ROOM

I found a house,
A very small house,
Actually it was more like a room.
The door was open,
It was bright inside,
Exciting, cheerful and bright colours of every kind.
There was pink, green, yellow and orange,
Black, white, purple and red.
The lines were fine,
Thick and thin lines.
Twirls and swirls,
Zigzags and boxes,
And rainbows up high in the sky.
If I was to have a room like this,
I wouldn't like it one bit.
With all those bright and beautiful colours
I would get no sleep at all.

Vicky Abbott (12)
Hassenbrook School

I AM WHAT I EAT

Why, oh why did I eat so much?
If only I could have saved myself,
I am what I eat!

The said fruit was healthy,
Not this fruit,
From the Garden of Eden,
I am what I eat!

I'll be like this forever,
Ever and ever,
Trapped in this body of evil,
I am what I eat!

I'm gloomy, sad, trapped!
I'm what I eat.
This is what I'll always be,
This is what I'll ever be.

What I ate!

Melanie Russell (12)
Hassenbrook School

NO ESCAPE

Trapped inside my mind
Thoughts everywhere
Surrounded by confusion
What next?
What's happening?

Visions rush through my head
What do they mean?
Why is it happening?
Surrounded by colours
Light everywhere

Imprisoned by my thoughts
I can't clear my mind
Loneliness, fear, worry
Different feelings everywhere
Excitement, confusion, pain

Trapped . . .
There's no escape!

Joanne Myler (13)
Hassenbrook School

THE CIGARETTE

I'm only a cigarette
A tiny little thing,
My packet says it all,
I'm mightier than a king.
I rule with an iron fist,
I boast no royal claim,
But I'm a star,
I'm famous,
As every corner shop sells my name.
Light me up,
Inhale my badness,
I'll dye your tongue,
I'll blacken your lungs,
And give you diseases far from happiness.
I'm a disaster ready to happen,
You drop me,
I ember,
You adore me,
I kill,
I am filled with the gift of cancer,
I will . . .

Jack Conway (12)
Hassenbrook School

DRINKING AND DRIVING

My favourite possession
Is in my car,
My pride and joy,
The best by far.

My favourite place,
Just has to be,
My local pub,
That's the place for me.

All my mates,
They never dare,
To drink and drive,
But I don't care.

I don't see a problem,
I've been doing it for years,
But they all say,
'It will end in tears.'

Drive to the pub,
Have a drink,
Only a few,
7 or 8 I think.

Time to go,
I get in my car,
I'm not drunk,
And it isn't far.

It's raining hard,
I can barely see,
Is that a person
Or is it a tree?

Where am I now?
The lights are bright,
I can't move,
It's really quiet.

The doc says,
They can fix my head,
But the man I hit,
Well, he is dead!

I have to live,
With what I have done,
At the time,
It seemed like fun.

Now I never drive,
And I never drink,
I learnt my lesson,
Too late I think.

Ian MacKenzie (12)
Hassenbrook School

A SUMMER'S WIND

A summer's wind wafts through a kitchen,
Gathering delicious smells of baking as it goes.
It swirls round flowers collecting exquisite perfumes as it travels.
It blows over a lake, rippling the water,
Drifting through trees, making leaves rustle.
It swoops over a hill and lifts up a kite, carrying it away.
Then, without warning it dies,
And disappears as suddenly as it came.

Charlotte Brainwood (11)
Hassenbrook School

GINGERBREAD MAN

They're looking at me,
They're looking at me,
Those men in the red and blue suits.
They're looking at me with hungry eyes,
Those men in the red and blue suits.

I'm a gingerbread man,
I'm a gingerbread man,
Laying here on the shelf.
I'm a gingerbread man with a great big smile,
Laying here on the shelf.

Come little girl,
come little girl,
Come and get me please.
Come little girl I'm waiting especially for you,
Come and get me please.

Oh Mr Builder,
Oh Mr Builder,
Please stop looking at me.
Oh Mr Builder please don't eat me for your tea,
Please stop looking at me.

There are cream cakes and currant cakes,
And all sorts of yummy cakes,
So please stop looking at me.
There are iced buns, jammy buns, all sorts of other buns,
Choose one of them for your tea.

You're getting closer,
You're getting closer,
You're coming through the door.
You're getting closer, closer to me,
And you're dropping mud on the floor.

Oh Mr Builder,
Oh Mr Builder,
Why did you have to choose me?
You've eaten my left leg,
You've eaten my right leg,
And now you're breaking my arms,
Why did you have to choose me?

Victoria King (13)
Hassenbrook School

NAUGHTY BUT NICE

D rip, drip, drip, the sound of the hungry builder's saliva
hitting the floor.
O is the shape of the doughnut. It makes it look nice with
sprinkles and the filling. It is so hard to resist.
U rk, urk, urk, the sound of his saliva being withdrawn in to
his saliva infested mouth.
G ruckel, gruckel, gruckel, the sound of the crumbs hitting
the dirt filled floor.
H urch, hurch, hurch, the sound of the builder's teeth
grinding together.
N urckl, nurckl, nurckl, the sound of the stomach growling
and luring him to the doughnut.
U rch, urch, urch, the sound of the builder sucking all the
doughnut filling that is stuck to his hand.
T urch, turch, turch, the sound of the builder stepping over
the crumbs as he departs.

Rachitha Perera (12)
Hassenbrook School

THE MIRROR OF NO REFLECTIONS

I looked in the mirror and saw my reflection,
I studied it hard. I was missing a section.
I strained my eyes, trying to see but I just couldn't
                                figure out what it could be.
Then I realised it was the flesh of me!
What's happening?
Is it a dream or is it real?
I wondered as I lay there still.
I heard a bellow from down the hall,
'Wake up Ria - it's time for school!'
Thank goodness, it was a dream after all!

Ria Crane (13)
Hassenbrook School

SHADOW OF DOUBT

Over the hill I sit and wait,
I am alone, but people are here.
I feel blocked out from the world I come from,
And the need so desperately to get back.
I cannot see but I know my surroundings,
I cannot touch, but I can feel.

Over the hill I sit and wait,
I am watching everything go by
And it's all in slow motion.
I am in a world of negative,
But I need to be positive.
The only way to get back is to use mental strength,
And this is very hard.

Over the hill I sit and wait,
I am climbing down, getting closer to my world.
I can see and I can touch,
At last I am back,
I am me again.

S J Kinch (12)
Hassenbrook School

THE FRUIT MAN

Beans for a moustache
Berries for hair
Only women can dream and stare
His luscious lips of cherries
His smooth skin of berries
I don't like the head as an avocado
It looks like the hump of the great Quasimodo
The pupils are juicy raspberries
His eye colour is ripe strawberries
Melon is the chest
Peaches are the cheeks
Eyebrows are wheat
He looks like a tasty man to meet
This is the man that I can see
The fruit man, the fruit man, the fruit man is he.

Jenna Hall (12)
Hassenbrook School

GRIM REAPER
(A POEM ABOUT CANCER)

Not a man
In a long, black cape.
Not a spirit,
Pure evil.
Not a person,
Not just a fear,
A reality
For one in three.

It starts off small,
A harmless child,
So good you hardly notice.
But it grows relentless,
Faster, faster,
A parasite murderer.

You can drug it, cut it, seemingly destroy it,
But it always finds the hiding place.
And when it comes
Out of hibernation
There's nothing you can do.

Bigger, bigger,
It grows and grows,
No being stands a chance.
A pointless battle, for when it wins
It ultimately loses.

Gemma Foster (14)
New Hall School

THE STALLION

A grey figure galloping in the distance
Caught my eye,
The horse seemed to dance,
I wish he was mine, I gave a sigh,
I do wish he was mine.

The riderless horse on the seashore
Pranced in the whipped up foam,
A tail as white as snow
Through the waves he tore,
I do wish he was mine.

I watched him till the sun set,
He became a light shadow,
Before I knew it, the foam set
And he was gone,
I do wish he was mine.

All night I thought about him,
It whirred around in my head,
I loved him, I saw him again,
But only in my head,
I do wish he was mine.

Rebecca Neal (11)
New Hall School

MY FUTURE

I would like to be a footballer, let the match begin.
I like to run with the ball,
I'm running down the pitch,
Then I score.
United are winning 1-0 against Liverpool.
Oh no, there they go again.
Beckham scored, United 2 Liverpool 0.
It is half-time.
The second half begins.
Giggs takes the whole defence and scored, United 3 Liverpool 0.
Owens shoots, a great save from Barthez.
Five minutes till full-time.
Veron scored, United 4 Liverpool 0.
One minute till full-time,
Cole scores, United 5 Liverpool 0.
It is full-time,
United are top of the league.

Ryon Hoyt (13)
The Hayward School

I'M A DOLPHIN

Splish, splash!
Splish, splash!
Won't you play with me?
I'm a dolphin
As beautiful as can be.
From up above you see me peek,
Under the water you hear me squeak.

Amy Hubbard (12)
The Hayward School

DOLPHINS

Dolphins in the deep blue sea
Diving for everyone to see.
Water splashes over everyone
As they watch and have lots of fun.

Dolphins are clever,
Jumping through hoops,
Doing their tricks makes people laugh.
Dolphins like treats of fish to eat.

Dolphins are friendly to people,
They let them ride on their backs.
Throw a fish in the water
And they can catch it.

I would love to swim with the dolphins,
I would like to play with them too.

Katie Beech (15)
The Hayward School

ZODIAC POEM 2

Capricorn the goat
Has a hairy coat.

Next Libra the scales,
Heads or tails.

Next is Cancer the crab,
Lives under a slab.

Alex Neville (11)
The Hayward School

KANE TOMBSTONE

Rock bottom.
The last raid.
The swanton bomb.
The stone cold stunner.
The pedigree.
An ankle lock.
With these moves
The Gore threw him into the table,
The more he did it, his head got sore.
He got the chokeslam from Kane.
He got his head rammed into a steel chair.
Kane won.

Damien Matthews (12)
The Hayward School

LIONS

Lions are yellow.
They are furry.
Leo is large.
He is looking in the jungle
For some meat.
He makes friends
With other lions.
Lions have no mummy and no daddy.

Laura Wolff (11)
The Hayward School

MY LITTLE KITTEN

My little kitten plays with his ball.
My little kitten gets tangled up in wool.
My little kitten stays up all night.
My little kitten he's a sight.
He runs up stairs, he runs in the room,
You should have seen him.
He runs with Dad,
He runs with Mum,
I think he's quite dumb.
My mum said, 'He is a crazy cat,
Why can't that cat sit on the mat?'

Louise Deigan (12)
The Hayward School

CATS

Cats are hissing,
Cats are spitting,
Unhappy cats,
Cats are miaowing,
Cats are purring,
Happy cats are in rubbish
Making a mess,
Naughty cats.

Vicky Louden (13)
The Hayward School

I HAVE A FRIEND

I have a friend and his name is Billy,
Because he is so silly.
He has a dog,
His name is Fred
Because he lies on the bed.
His mum has a big gum and she is so dumb.
When he and I go to the shop
And we buy something he goes pop.
I do nothing.

Luke Benson (13)
The Hayward School

DOGS

Dogs thin, dogs fat,
Dogs white, dogs black.
Dogs love to run about,
They bark as if they shout.
Dogs look up in the sky
When it brightens,
They bark if they are frightened,
And when they hear a rumble of thunder
Their ears point up
And they run for cover!

Jamie Frost (15)
The Hayward School